The Hudson River Valley

The Henry Hudson Monument, Riverdale.

The Hudson River Valley

BY JOHN REED

BONANZA BOOKS / NEW YORK

This edition is published by Bonanza Books, a division of Crown Publishers, Inc.,
by arrangement with Clarkson N. Potter, Inc.
B C D E F G H

Library of Congress Card Catalogue Number: 60-8925

For Phyllis

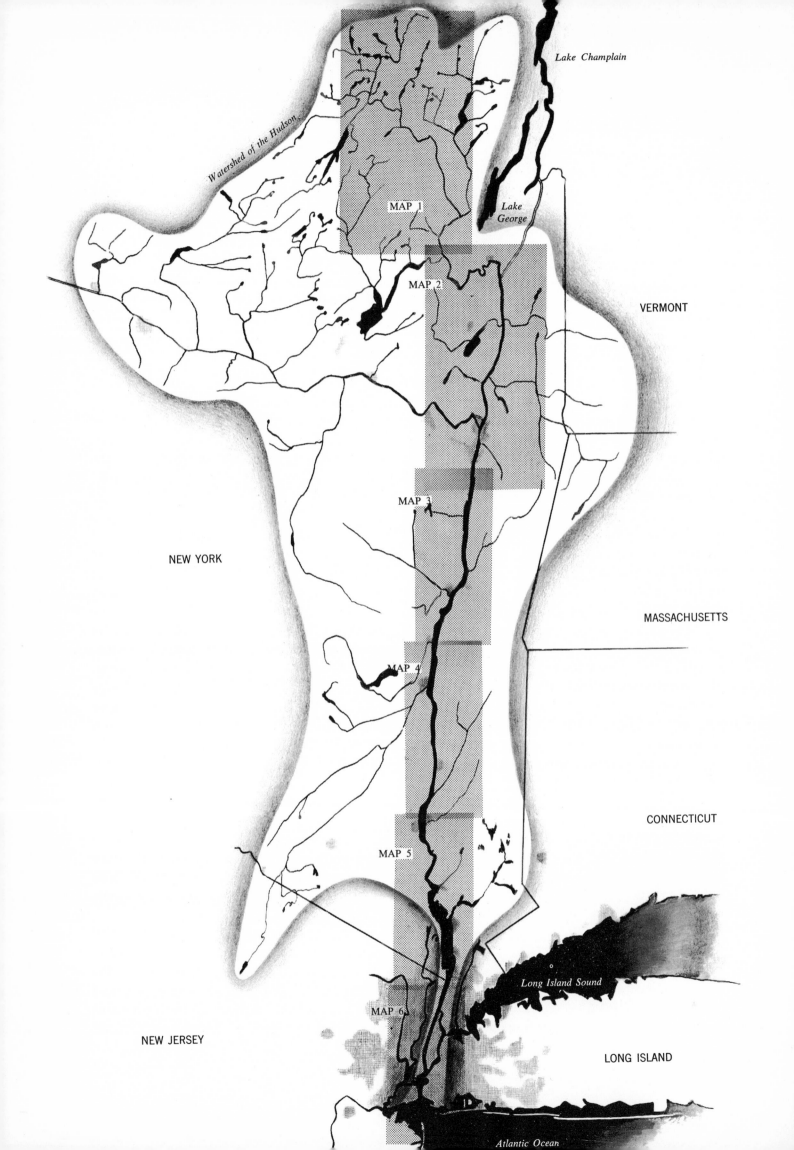

Watershed of the Hudson

Lake Champlain

Lake George

MAP 1

MAP 2

VERMONT

MAP 3

NEW YORK

MASSACHUSETTS

MAP 4

MAP 5

CONNECTICUT

Long Island Sound

MAP 6

NEW JERSEY

LONG ISLAND

Atlantic Ocean

A hundred years ago the river was central in the life of many American communities. In those days steamboats were the best means of transporting most goods, the luxurious way to travel, the harbingers of news and excitement, and the links by which the whole length of a river would be held together as one community. Up and down the navigable channel the great boats raced, and just as surely as the waters from the lands around flowed down to the river, so did all the products of farmer and manufacturer.

In time, the railways came and the steamships disappeared. The towns that had faced the river gradually changed their aspects and left the waterfronts to chemical plants and decay. Then the automobile added to people's mobility, and the network of railways and highways spread out in an over-all pattern that could generally ignore the valley of a stream. Railways still frequently followed the river—they border the Hudson on both sides, running just a few feet from the water for hundreds of miles—but they did so only for the advantage of the level route laid for them by nature. The water might just as well not be there.

Today the river is in most ways peripheral to the life of the communities upon its banks. A portion of their products and supplies may still come and go on the river, but it is a small portion, except in the case of the large ports near its mouth where the river is a roadstead and a harbor. The towns have moved up the hills. The giant speedways swing free of its shores and plunge through their comparative isolation to well-marked destinations. Most of the great homes have gone or have been made into institutions. All of these changes have taken place in the Hudson River valley.

And yet, the Hudson is one of the great rivers.

The Hudson is a small river in America, a smaller one in the world. The Rhine, to which it is so often compared, is twice its length, and the Rhine is not among the giant rivers that give rise along their lengths to entire civilizations or mark subcontinents with their agricultural and geographic unity. The Hudson is not at all a Ganges or a Congo, nor even a Mekong or a Missouri, rivers that have grown over vast areas and have made enormous plains where once mountains rose. These rivers flow through their last hundreds of miles in great sluggish loops amid fertile fields and everything on either side is dependent to some extent upon their existence, their floods, and their commerce.

The Hudson is not a river whose banks contain the shards of an ancient civilization and all the centuries of history and fable since. It is a new river in a new land that, before Henry Hudson, had for its history only the fishing and hunting and warfare of the Indians, who lived in the unvarying pattern of primitive life and did not create events of historical interest as we understand them. Nearly all of what we read in ordinary history are the accounts of struggles between states and peoples, and there is relatively little of this in the life of the Hudson. There were frontier struggles and clashes among the colonizing Europeans that were important in the development of this country, and sometimes vital to the future of the European powers concerned. These are often fascinating as personal exploits, but generally they involved only a few very brave or desperate or avaricious individuals along with a few-score Indian enemies or allies; important as these may have been to the region, they were actually no more than the small-scale conflicts of any frontier.

The events of the American Revolution were few in number along its shores and, except for one or two actions, relatively minor in deciding the struggle. The loss of New York City to the British early in the war was important, if only because thereafter the threat to cut the colonies in two was ever present. The full-scale battle of Saratoga was certainly one of the important engagements of the Revolution; it not only decisively flung back a large British invasion from Canada, but it also consolidated American resistance and enormously raised American morale. And, coming when it did, had Arnold's attempted betrayal of West Point been successful, it might have been as important as any revolutionary engagement along the river. The rest of the skirmishes and the long stalemates were minor though often necessary parts of the campaign. Since those days the river has been part of a community whose security has not been touched directly by war and whose only historic sites and monuments commemorating gallant actions and decisive battles are therefore all very old indeed to us, although they are still less than two hundred years old.

This small new river, without ancient landmarks and obscure in a large country and a great continent, nevertheless has an attraction that is out of proportion with everything about it except its beauty and its unique quality of being a great river—a distinction it achieves in a mere three hundred twenty miles. Along the eastern coast of North America there is but one great river, the St. Lawrence, which is nearly a thousand miles long and opens its funnel slowly to the width of one hundred miles or more in an imperceptible blending with the ocean. From the St. Lawrence to the Mississippi there are no great rivers, and even in this company of the small waterways of the east coast the Hudson is not the longest.

But the Hudson is not typical. Its cliffs and hills, its mile-wide glitter opposite Manhattan, its Catskills and Adirondacks looming into cloud forms at evening, the strange sight of its bright freighters moving swiftly and surely so far from the ocean, its cliff-scaling roads and tall bridges, its inland sea some fifteen miles long and an average three miles wide—all are parts of a river different from those to the north and south of it. The Susquehanna, which is one hundred fifty miles longer than the Hudson, dissipates its strength, splays out in low country into a wide, rocky, and shallow bed, and empties into the upper reaches of a great bay, still one hundred fifty miles from the sea. The Delaware chatters over stones in its shallow course until it is a few-score miles from Wilmington, which is itself tucked seventy-five miles from the ocean at Cape May. The James, the Roanoke, and the Connecticut do not take seagoing vessels inland to their cities, and in fact have few cities along their courses. They all flow from their sources, often in beauty through the logical valleys made by their waters, drop fast over rocks, sometimes flood wide over farm lands, and are, in short, the quite handsome, typical rivers of Eastern America.

But the Hudson is more.

The first reason for this is that it was once a much larger river than it now is, and that the character of its past is evident in its surroundings as well as in its own great breadth and depth.

Much of the Hudson valley is that of an ice-age river within which the smaller, newer Hudson has cut its channel; the bed of the river is below sea level for almost half its total length. In this long and remarkably straight part of its course, unencumbered by falls or rapids, the waters of the Hudson drop very slowly south, not steadily, but in an intricate push of water against the tides, which twice daily reverse the flow of the river for many miles and slow it and raise its level as far north as Troy, one hundred seventy miles from its mouth. This slow, reversing current, along with its depth, gives the Hudson the qualities of a fiord.

The Mohawks called the Hudson "Oiogue," meaning the beautiful river, and a river's beauty is its setting. The Hudson flows out of old mountains as picturesquely jumbled as any in the East, then flows through spacious, fertile valleys, first dammed and locked, then free and island-studded. Distant mountains and long embracing bluffs adorn its middle passages. Steep, beetling mountains press close, then fall away as the wide Tappan Zee swells out below them. Finally the Hudson's unique palisades of rock follow down to the great harbors with their many interlocking straits and peninsulas.

The Hudson River is a great river first by the grace of nature.

The Hudson comes from an area that is a splatter of blue on the map, a tangle of lakes and rivers among wooded hills and a few red lines of roads. Wriggling through the center of the Adirondacks, it is also in the midst of several difficulties of nomenclature and identification, and its own name and source are among them.

There is no question that the central core of the Adirondacks, having been thrust up from the sea more than a billion years ago, is as old as any rock in the world. Though but foothills of their antique selves, the peaks surrounding the Hudson's sources are among the highest mountains in the East. But according to the best deductions that can be made from the ancient geological jumble, these glacier-worn mountains are different from the younger Appalachians, which surround them. They are, it seems, a southern outcropping of the much older Canadian Laurentians.

The 5344 feet of rounded Mt. Marcy, on whose slopes the Hudson rises, clearly establish it as the tallest mountain between New Hampshire and southwest Virginia. But its name has been a cause for argument for more than a century. When Ebenezer Emmons, a famous geologist appointed in 1836 by Governor Marcy to survey the region, first climbed the mountain it was apparently nameless. His experienced guide, John Cheney, knew of no name for it and Emmons had to refer to the mountains as "The Highest Peak of Essex" (County). He named it Marcy. A few weeks later a New York journalist who had rushed to climb Marcy as far as his single leg would permit wrote that, although it was perhaps only proper to name it for the governor who had made the expedition possible, the more poetic Indian word meaning "cloud-splitter," would hardly be an extravagant description of the grandeur of the mountain. From this suggestion of Charles Hoffman the legend grew that the beautiful old Indian name, Tahawus, had indeed been discarded for a politician's.

The Hudson first flows through the center of a park that is larger than any national park, any other state park, and all but one national forest. Yet it is only half park. The "Blue Line" surrounding the Adirondack State Park encloses five million acres of land, but slightly more than half of these consist of mines, elaborate and costly camps and clubs, commercial lumber tracts, hotels, farms, and ski centers, and many other private properties that are mixed with the forest

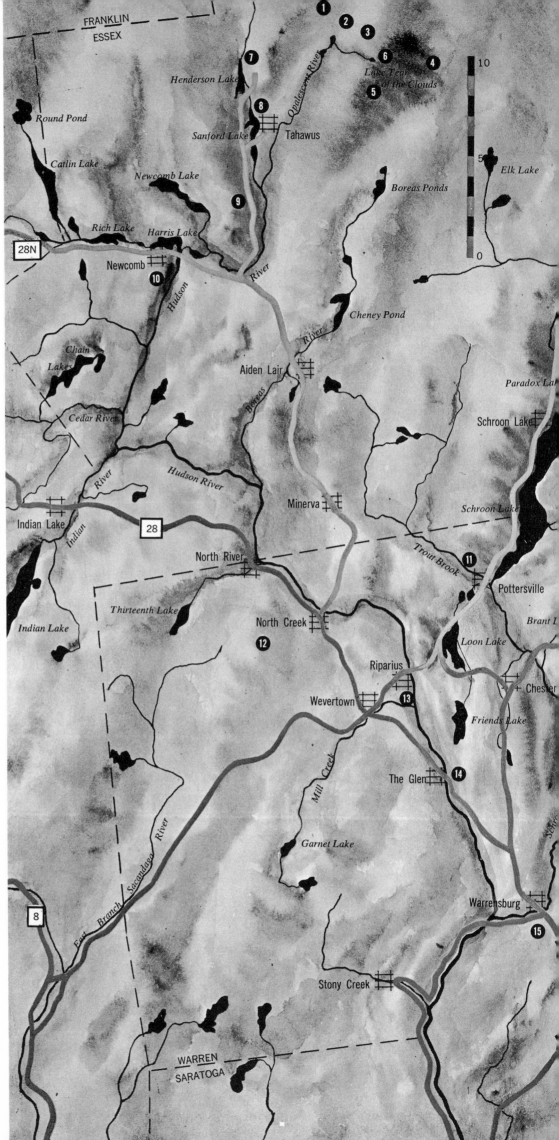

Note: Italics indicate that there is a photograph. Except for octagonal houses, which are grouped on pages 174-5, all relevant photographs are arranged from north to south in an order closely following the numbers of the maps.

MAP 1:

SOURCE TO STONY CREEK

1. Mt. MacIntyre, 5,112′
2. Mt. Colden, 4,713′
3. Mt. Marcy, 5,344′
4. Mt. Haystack, 4,918′
5. Mt. Skylight, 4,920′
6. *Lake Tear, source of Hudson*
7. *Henderson Lake, source of the Hudson*
8. *Open pit titanium mine, mills, and company town*
9. *First of the lumber mills of the upper river*
10. Newcomb, once a center of the lumber industry
11. Stone bridge and caves
12. Garnet mine, for 50 years the country's greatest source of garnets
13. The widening river, *view south near Riparius*
14. *View south from the bridge*
15. *Warrensburg,* the first mills

preserves throughout the area. The park that was established to keep this wild area wild is filled with perhaps more industrial and commercial enterprises, homes and resorts than any other.

Finally, there is the odd beginning of the Hudson. Lake Tear of the Clouds, which once bore the less flowery name of Summit Water, is a tiny, spring-fed pond on the slopes of Mt. Marcy. At 4293 feet above sea level it is the highest source in New York State from which water continually flows to the ocean. It is invariably described as the source of the Hudson, sometimes being further qualified as the highest and most northerly source. This qualification would seem to be necessary because the stream that flows westward from Lake Tear is called Feldspar Brook, and the river that this and other brooks make is named the Opalescent River. Only after some fifteen miles of modest existence under these names do these waters join a river that flows down from the north out of Henderson Lake and beyond, and that detailed maps label the Hudson River. Generally the name of a river follows along its diminishing branches according to the whim of its first explorers or later legislation, and wherever the name leads the river winds to its source. But in the Adirondacks the name of the Hudson flows down one stream and the waters of its most popular source flow down another.

Like a visual chart of all this confusion, the young river at first plunges briefly in every direction but north, one among a thousand other streams threading the Adirondacks. For some thirty-five miles of its chattering youth the Hudson tumbles through the forests with no road winding along its banks, a length of loneliness not to be repeated. It is joined by the Goodnow, Cedar, Indian, and Boreas rivers, with waters from the slopes of mountains bearing such names as Blue, Calamity, Dun Brook, Skylight, Bad Luck, Kunjamuk, Kettle, Ruby, and Vanderwhacker, and from ponds and lakes named Mink, Split Rock, Pickwacker, Little Moose, and Unknown. The area has much in common with the upper reaches of many streams of the Northeast, but the variety of features—lakes, ponds, cliffs, hills, rivers, meadows, forests—liable to be crammed into a few miles often makes it as picturesque as its names. (Among the hundreds of hills and mountains of the park there are 1345 named lakes.)

Emerging alongside a highway, the Hudson comes down to North River, a tiny town, and to North Creek, and now it has grown to a wide though shallow stream and wanders less wildly, flowing through a spacious valley toward the south. It is joined by two more rivers, one, the Schroon, carrying the waters of the some seven hundred square miles or more between the Hudson and Lakes George and Champlain. The other flows only a few miles from Sacandaga Reservoir, as large as Lake George and fed by all the streams in the thousand square miles between the Hudson and the Mohawk.

Now the river is a hundred miles long. It has been part of a wilderness, half natural and half maintained by logging properties and forest preserves. The towns along the banks of the Hudson have all been small. Their people work mostly as guides and hosts to fishermen and campers and skiers, as small farmers, merchants, miners, and lumbermen. Many more Adirondack natives were lumbermen a hundred years ago when the forests were floating down-river to the mills in such masses that the state led the nation in the production of lumber. Even then, the flow of water from the northern streams was diminishing as the trees were felled. When a process was discovered for making paper pulp of the spruce that had sprung up in the wake of logging and the smaller trees that had been left, a second lumbering boom began and by 1900 the state was a leading producer of paper. The rivers and creeks became even smaller until the establish-

MAP 2:

LUZERNE TO ALBANY

1. *A small gorge;* the river is dammed for power
2. Palmer, logs in the back yards
3. *Glens Falls, paper mills*
4. Home and grave of Jane McCrea
5. Mt. McGregor, Ulysses S. Grant's cottage
6. *Farmland,* melons and cattle
7. *Schuyler house,* 1777, and Saratoga monument
8. Racing museum
9. Skidmore College
10. Race tracks
11. Bemis Heights, Battle of Saratoga, 1777
12. Fort Johnson, 1749, and Johnson Hall, 1762, homes of William Johnson at Johnstown and Amsterdam
13. *Octagonal house*
14. *Bennington battlefield,* 1777
15. *Burnt Hills, winter*
16. Large paper mill
17. Union College
18. *Shaker community and graveyard*
19. Rensselaer Polytechnic Institute
20. Emma Willard School
21. *State Capitol*
22. Schuyler Mansion, 1762
23. Fort Crailo, 1642

ment of the park saved the remaining stands of timber. Although the forests are growing again, thanks to reforestation and a much smaller, regulated lumber industry, the streams can no longer carry logs as they once did each spring. Fortunately, they are not needed, for today railroads and trucks not only are more economical but they can also haul the heavier hardwood logs that could not be floated down the rivers.

The towns grow a little larger as the hills grow smaller. Mills at Warrensburg and Luzerne Falls use the river water in making paper and cloth. At Corinth the river arrives at a town of some three thousand and, as though it were time, the river turns sharply to the east and leaves the park.

At once the river is harnessed. Now sometimes three or four hundred feet wide but not yet a thoroughfare, it is dammed several times in an exceptionally tortuous twenty miles. There are dams and paper mills in Palmer and Glens Falls, and between the two towns the river is blocked a few times again where power stations hum in the solitude of pine woods. In Palmer the wood is piled in a vast yard full of railroad tracks, making a series of little mountains that loom high over the houses and stores of the main street.

As the river turns sharply south again at Fort Edward it flows into a widening valley of farms and small, quiet towns. The country rolls far off to the Vermont hills and the river widens between stands of popular, oak, and birch. From here to Troy the water lies quietly in miles-long ponds between locks because now the river is also a canal, a part of the waterway to Canada. The Champlain Canal leads northeast from the Hudson at Fort Edward to Lake Champlain and the Richelieu River continues on from the long lake to the St. Lawrence at Sorel.

The river continues for thirty miles past Schuylerville, where the Phillip Schuyler mansion is one of several fine old houses. It flows past Bemis Heights (where General Gates, accused of looking like a midwife by Burgoyne, replied that he was indeed one since he had delivered Burgoyne of five thousand men) and then runs on to aptly named Stillwater. On the east the roads run back to other small towns in the midst of fine dairy farms and cultivated fields. On the west the roads converge toward the old resort of Saratoga Springs.

In Saratoga as early as 1790 crude taverns housed a few guests who sought the benefits of the waters the Indians had long known. The town had a remarkably swift growth—a three-story hotel and three coach lines by 1815, facilities for one thousand guests by 1825, railways in 1833 —and a long-lasting popularity. Everyone had to see Saratoga and nearly everyone did, including Lafayette, Irving, Cooper, Southern planters with eligible daughters, race-track touts, every statesman of the day, English critics, and gamblers. For more than a century Saratoga was a rich mixture of society, sport, and sin. The ornate hotels with their verandas and luxurious cottages and dining halls are gone now, but Saratoga still has beautiful or exuberantly Victorian buildings, fine race tracks, the now state-owned springs (with strangely medieval-looking areas of regimented pines), and its lake in the midst of gently rolling country.

The Hoosic River wanders out of northwest Massachusetts into Vermont. Another branch flows from Bennington, past the battlefield where Stark ambushed five hundred of Burgoyne's Hessians, and joins the main river, which enters the Hudson just below Stillwater. Then Mechanicville, by its name and the plumes of smoke from the tall chimneys of its paper mill, announces the approaching change in the river country. After a few more miles a second canal, at Waterford, marks the close of this rural life along the Hudson. Just above the natural confluence of the two rivers, the Barge Canal in about one and one-half miles lifts its traffic one hundred sixty-nine feet through five locks from the Hudson to the level of the Mohawk. It is only the beginning of its climb toward the West. The canal follows the Mohawk more than one hundred miles, then is joined to Lake Oneida and, through natural and man-made courses, extends a total distance of three hundred fifty miles to Lake Erie, five hundred sixty-five feet higher than the Hudson. Two hundred years ago, the nearer parts of the Mohawk valley were the first areas to be settled as a tentative extension westward from the protection of the Hudson, and this largest of its tributaries flows past its own varied store of handsome country and historic sites.

Waterford is the outpost of the first urban complex of the river. South and west of here in a triangle lie three cities: Schenectady is on the Mohawk fifteen miles to the west; Troy and Albany are seven miles apart on the Hudson. Smaller towns—Cohoes, Watervliet, Rensselaer, Menands, Scotia—lie adjacent to the three large ones, bringing the total population in the industrial triangle to some four hundred thousand people. Railroad tracks border the river's banks and lace the map in every direction.

The northern linchpin of the Hudson, which also stands at the only real opening through the Appalachian barrier to the West, was destined from the beginning to be a center of trade and industry. The earliest settlement on the river, the Dutch fort and fur-trading post at Albany became the first American city in 1686. Upstream, the rapids and falls of both its rivers provided power for its mills and made it the northern terminus for sail and steamboats alike. After 1825 De Witt Clinton's big ditch carried almost all the products of the West to the factories and ports of the East, of which the three cities of the triangle enjoyed being first. Their manufactured goods also had cheap and rapid transportation back to the expanding market. Here the first steam powered train in America ran from Albany to Schenectady in 1831, and by 1867 Commodore Vanderbilt's driving ambition had forged a single system from New York to Buffalo by way of the Hudson and Mohawk valleys.

The wealth of the region is purchased at the cost of industrial ugliness. There are expensive homes and tree-lined suburban streets, and handsome small towns are set among the dairy farms of the neighboring country, but the cities themselves are largely warrens of factories and warehouses. The century-old, narrow-windowed brick mills and foundries of local families sometimes have new additions to match the steel and glass style of the modern corporation. Albany has the parks of its capitol area, and far-flung suburbs stretch out between Albany and Schenectady. Both cities also contain many extremely handsome old houses in their downtown areas, some of which are prized and preserved. But Troy and most of the smaller centers along the river have little that relieves the dark pattern of the mill town. Industrial decentralization is now setting factories in their parks out in the green country, but the grimy nineteenth-century concentration down along the river remains largely unchanged. The more open, cleaner lines of modern power and planning are handsomely used, however, in Albany's large new port below the city, set among fields of oil tanks waiting to be filled from the ships that lie nose to stern along the quay.

Change is the characteristic of such an area, of course, but a few buildings remain from the eighteenth and early nineteenth centuries. The fortified stone house of the first Dutch patroon, lord of seven hundred thousand acres, still faces the river, clinging to a narrow lot in Rensselaer after more than two hundred fifty years. Kitty Rensselaer crossed the river before the Revolution to become mistress of Philip Schuyler's handsome residence on the hill south of Albany. There Burgoyne would enjoy the famous hospitality of his recent opponent, and there young Alexander Hamilton would marry her daughter, Elizabeth. And in the very center of the triangle, in a last patch of country surrounded by the wide-fanning suburbia, stand the last few houses of the Shakers, that strict, celibate sect that first built here in 1792, attracted thousands to its ranks and then declined, leaving a hardy few to survive into the middle of the impervious twentieth century.

From this point on the Hudson is really a fiord rather than a river. In its first one hundred fifty miles the river rushed down from its highest source at 4293 feet, and dropped to 128 feet above sea level at the decisive southward turn near Fort Edward—ninety-seven per cent of its fall to the sea before it is even halfway there. At Troy the Hudson has come forty more miles, and here where it passes the last dam in its course its mean elevation above the ocean, which lies more than one hundred fifty miles farther south, is less than two feet. The river lies now in the basin of an older Hudson valley that started where the river left the foothills of the Adirondacks; its bed is now well below sea level.

The Hudson is a fiord or estuary because it was once a much larger river. The waters from the last glaciers poured down from the north cutting a wide, deep valley and flowing out to a much lower sea than that of today. The later Hudson, then, is a "drowned valley," that part of the ancient river's course that is below the present sea level. South of the federal lock at Troy the river does not flow out into the sea by gravity; it is pushed out by the supply of fresh waters from its upper branches and from all the creeks and kills and springs along the rest of its course that perpetually fill the long, deep fiord to overflowing.

The tides travel all the way to Troy, a slow surge up the river that gives the waters a saline content and reverses the current for many miles. An Algonquin legend is said to have explained their generations of wandering toward the east as a search for a river that flowed two ways. At the Hudson they at last found their promised river and spread their villages along its banks. Of course, Algonquins covered a large part of Canada, too, but perhaps it was the Iroquois who persuaded them to abandon their search. In any case the name is apt: The-River-That-Flows-Two-Ways.

Below Albany, the Hudson begins to increase in size. It shortly becomes an average half mile wide or more, at first broad but shallow with numerous islands and sluggish necks of water. It is a barrier of considerable importance, however, and it will become more difficult to bridge as it goes south. In the fifty miles between Glens Falls and Albany twelve bridges span the river; in the one hundred fifty miles remaining there are only nine.

North of the Catskills we are still in the wide, agricultural valley. It is a land of small towns along the gentle bluffs that are beginning to border the river, towns that have sometimes the peaceful atmosphere of an earlier America, with the implied decline of local trade and industry, and towns that have sometimes the ugly qualities of the rural slum.

Scattered along the river north of Hudson are some old houses, none very grand, but often beautifully set in the gentle scene. The last of the huge and blocky old icehouses stand at the water's edge, black against the hills behind them. Once they were thick on either shore, some of them as large as three hundred fifty feet by two hundred seventy feet and thirty or forty feet

MAP 3:

CASTLETON TO SAUGERTIES

1. *Shaker communities at New Lebanon and Shaker Village,* and Shaker Museum at Old Chatham
2. *Brickyards*
3. *House of History*
4. Lindenwald, early 19th-century, Martin Van Buren
5. *Beginnings of the Catskills*
6. *Nutten Hook*
7. *Thirteen-sided barn*
8. *Ice house*
9. *Octagonal house*
10. Abram Stoat house, 1654
11. Parade on a bluff *overlooking the river*
12. Hudson City lighthouse
13. *Mt. Merino, view north* (view south from this point is the dust jacket picture)
14. Van Rensselaer south manor house
15. *Thomas Cole's house*
16. *Rip Van Winkle Bridge*
17. *Olana Castle,* late 19th-century, Frederick Church
18. *Catskill Mountain house*
19. Oak Hill, 1793, John Livingston
20. Iron Mountain Storage Vaults, maximum safety in what were the Burden Iron Mines
21. Clermont, 1730, the chief Livingston house, rebuilt after British troops burned it in 1777
22. Taconic hills, *view to river*
23. *Mills on Esopus Creek*

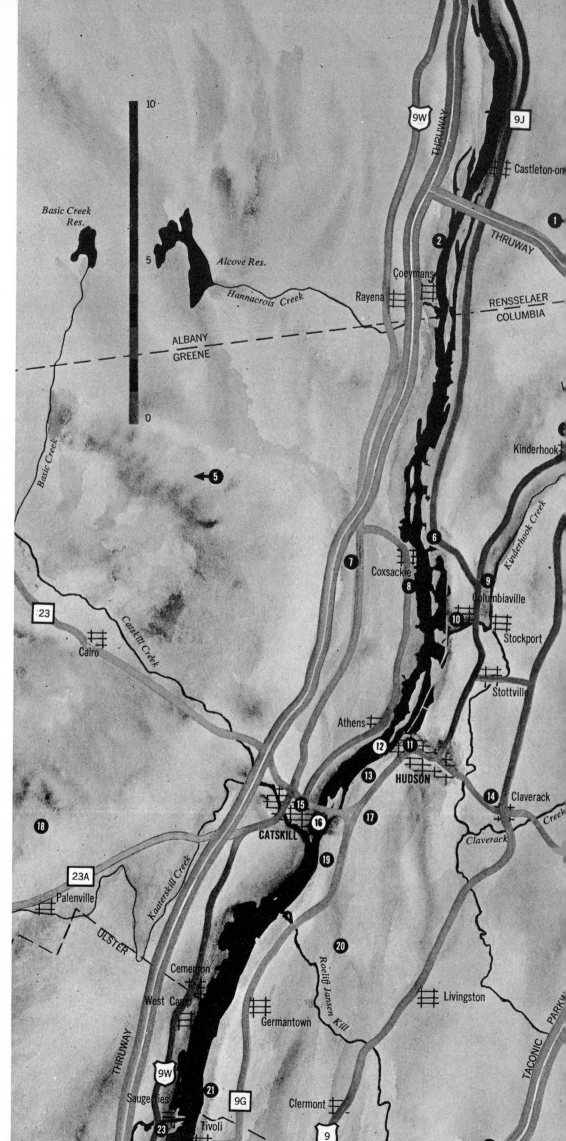

high. When the ice was ten inches or more in thickness local farmers and hired help would work with the regular crews at cutting and floating the slabs down dark canals to the conveyors that carried them up into the big storage barns. It was the winter crop of the river and its harvesting was a lively, pretty picture asking for a Bruegel who never came, continuing sometimes even at night, with torches set on poles in the glittering ice.

It's an area that has seen several industries come and go. As the country shot up in its adolescence, building materials were consumed at an enormous rate. There was bluestone, the extra hard sandstone found in the Catskill country, for buildings and pavings and curbs. The blue clay in deposits all along the river from below Albany almost to New York made fine bricks. Drying sheds once lay along the river for miles, and bricks in millions went down-river to build that ever-growing city at its mouth, or up-river and out to the West to build the bank and the banker's house in the frontier town and everything this side of it. There are still a few brickyards working on the west shore up-river, but most of them are clusters of roofless walls amid the reeds and sumac of the flats. Cement, too, was discovered in the hills of Ulster County. The discovery brought Irish, Dutch, and Yankees who turned the small towns into boom camps. For decades slow-drying Rosendale cement was favored for its ultra-hardness and was used in many large projects, including the Brooklyn Bridge. Faster-drying cements closed down the Hudson River mines for a time, but today the sheds of the modern cement plants flourish in their white landscapes from Albany to Saugerties. In the hills near Kingston a labyrinth of cement caves is now used for mushroom growing. The last icehouses happen to serve the same purpose.

Not all the industries of these countries have vanished, although the tanning of hides brought up the Hudson from South America also ceased on the west shore when the essential supply of hemlock bark came to an end in mid-century. The production of gypsum, for instance, goes on in a dozen plants in this area. As one looks toward the river from the Taconic Parkway, down over the pleasant countryside whose hills are dotted with dairy farms and the quilted patterns of orchards, the columns of smoke from the cement and gypsum factories will be seen punctuating the massed, dark Catskills behind them. Gypsum is found in several other areas along the river and its tributaries; at Cheshire Reservoir in Massachusetts, where the Hoosic River starts, a gypsum plant sits, huge and white from its own dust, on a hill above the sparkling lake, and another sprawls far south on the Hudson at Grassy Point.

Nor were all the industries on the west bank. The town of Hudson, an early center of manufacturing that still has cement plants and knitting mills, was founded late in the eighteenth century by Nantucket and New Bedford whalers whose fleet of twenty-five vessels was the largest of any river town. And after the stimulus provided when the country had to manufacture instead of import during the war of 1812, mills were set up in many small towns where streams tumbled down to the Hudson. Stockport Creek is typical. Wandering from the hills north of Lebanon, where numerous buildings of a Shaker community still stand, it passes through Malden Bridge, Chatham Center, Valatie, Kinderhook, Newton Hook, and Columbiaville, and in most of these small communities a long and narrow brick mill of a hundred years ago, three or four stories tall on the street side and five or six tall on the river side below the dam, stands with dark and glassless windows.

Where Stockport Creek flows into the river a few miles north of Hudson there is a different sort of building. Here, where Hudson made a landing on September 12, 1609, Abraham Stoat, less than fifty years later, built his house of stone and wood in the midst of the wilderness. After three centuries the solid Dutch structure still serves well as a home.

In addition to the timely discoveries of more resources on the west shore, other factors were at work to make for the differences between the east and west sides of the river, the differences that began early and are still noticeable today. In these parts the river flows past lands that were once enormous grants, the first being the Van Rensselaer properties. The Dutch patroon successfully evaded the limitations of his grant, extending his holdings until they measured more than twenty miles along the river and spread back on both sides until their total length was about forty-five miles east to west. The outlines of this tract are roughly contiguous with the boundaries of the present Albany and Rensselaer counties. The Van Rensselaer claims may have been much modified by the growth in their midst of Fort Orange (Albany), which was under the protection of the Dutch West India Company, but the family seemed to have balanced this invasion by even further claims in other directions. At Claverack, fifteen miles below their supposed property line, there was a house to which Van Rensselaer tenants delivered a shore of their produce as rent.

This house was just at the edge of the next great land grant along the river, that of Robert Livingston, the Scottish clerk who married the widow of Nicolaes Van Rensselaer—who was herself a Schuyler—and obtained one hundred sixty thousand acres from James II. The property of the powerful Livingston family was appropriately shaped like a keystone; about twelve miles apart on the river, the east-west boundaries fanned out until they were about twenty-four miles apart at the Connecticut and Massachusetts lines. This is the lower half of the present Columbia County. Several handsome old homes of various branches of the family overlook the river below the town of Hudson, including Clermont, the estate of the famous Chancellor Robert Livingston, rebuilt after the British raiders fired the beautiful stone mansion during the Revolution.

Only a part of the Rensselaer properties and the briefly held grant of a Captain Evans were on the west shore. Below Rensselaerwyck, the Catskills began on the west. The gentler country across the river was better land for farming. South of the Catskills there are miles of farm country before the highlands but no manor lords set up on either side of the river between the Livingstons and the several royal grants in Westchester. The east side of the river was first profitable, then fashionable. Except for the region from Kingston to Newburgh, the west shore was largely wilderness well into the nineteenth-century. Then its industries made it profitable too, but did nothing to make it fashionable. Of course, no more than all industry has remained on the west have all the large estates been built on the east of the river, but nearly all the colonial rich and most of those who made fortunes in the nineteenth-century had their homes there. As Schuyler married Rensselaer, and Livingstons allied with New York merchants and lawyers such as the Beekmans and Prendergasts, so the families who made their fortunes later were also often linked to the older up-river aristocracy by marriage, which sometimes decided where they would build their cottages and castles.

South of Hudson, then, where the river turns slightly west and the Taconic hills begin to rise over toward Connecticut, there begins an area in which are imbedded—usually off side roads and at the ends of long unimproved drives winding through thick woods—a great many of the large estates of the eighteenth and nineteenth-centuries. Nearly all of them command beautiful views across the river to the Catskill Mountains ten or twelve miles distant. North of Barrytown a good many of these houses are still the private homes of Livingstons and allied families. One

18

of the most fascinating is hilltop Olana Castle, a nineteenth-century version of a Persian palace built as a home and studio by the painter Frederick Church. It incorporates in its walls, windows, doors, and furnishings a wide variety of oriental materials collected by the artist during his travels in the Middle East. Directly across the river in Catskill lived the most famous of his fellow artists of the Hudson River school, Thomas Cole. The novelist and playwright Gore Vidal now lives in a handsome house built as a wedding present for a Livingston girl in 1820. The nearby huge white Donaldson house called Blithedale, once a center of social events in a time when lantern-festooned lawns and rowing on the river were popular, is now one of the buildings of Bard College. And when Blithedale's guests went for an evening of song on the river, they often rowed along past the point where the ruins that John Cruger had constructed looked as romantic in the moonlight as they were meant to. These incomplete walls and arches, which once sheltered pre-Columbian Mayan carvings, still stand, but Cruger's house, stables, and extensive gardens have vanished except for a few yards of foundation among the trees.

Montgomery Place, the home of the young general who left his bride of two years to lead the vain attack on Quebec in 1775, also stands on a hill near the river in Anandale. With its lawns and fine old trees it is doubtless as handsome as it was in 1818 when Richard Montgomery's widow, long since grown old, watched while the boats escorting the general's body to an honored grave in St. Pauls churchyard in New York City paused far below on the river to fire their cannon.

Most of the houses in this area and those immediately to the south, belonging to Chanlers, Delanos, Merritts, Astors, Roosevelts, and others, have not been converted into institutions, as have most of those across the river and farther south, but are still maintained as private estates. There are three houses above Poughkeepsie, however, that are open to the public. The best known is the home of Franklin Roosevelt, with the President's grave, the library, and the remarkably comfortable old house that attracts thousands of visitors each year. The village of Hyde Park takes its name from the first of several estates that have occupied the site on its north since 1705, now known as the Vanderbilt Mansion. In grounds of exquisite planting, the Italian Renaissance palace stands, as formal as the Roosevelt house is informal, on a hill between its own little Crum Elbow Creek and the river. Still farther north, the Ogden Mills estate is something like a stucco echo of the Vanderbilt marble. The slope to the river here is more gradual and a wide lawn flows down for hundreds of yards from the house and the odd pieces of statuary around it.

A house that is quite different from any of those on the east of the Hudson was built in 1823 behind the town of Catskill on the brink of the first sharp escarpment of the mountains. Today a shambles, the winds dismantling further each week the tall Corinthian columns of its veranda where the famous of America and Europe stood and tried to describe the scene below, the Catskill Mountain House was once considered to offer the visitor a spectacle the equal of Niagara. It is almost as great a wonder that thousands completed the climb to see the river valley laid like a map at their feet. Until an inclined railway was run up the face of the mountain in 1892, visitors were hauled in carriages from Catskill past the Sleepy Hollow near Palenville where Irving's Rip Van Winkle slept, up a rocky gorge cut into the mountains by a small creek, at the top of which they would then turn east to be jostled over the tops of the mountains to the precipice. The rigors of the round trip of more than thirty miles can be understood even today in the steep, winding canyon, and most of all when the last unpaved mile has been traversed. The Mountain House is abandoned, its ornate interiors are lathe and plaster, but from it on a clear

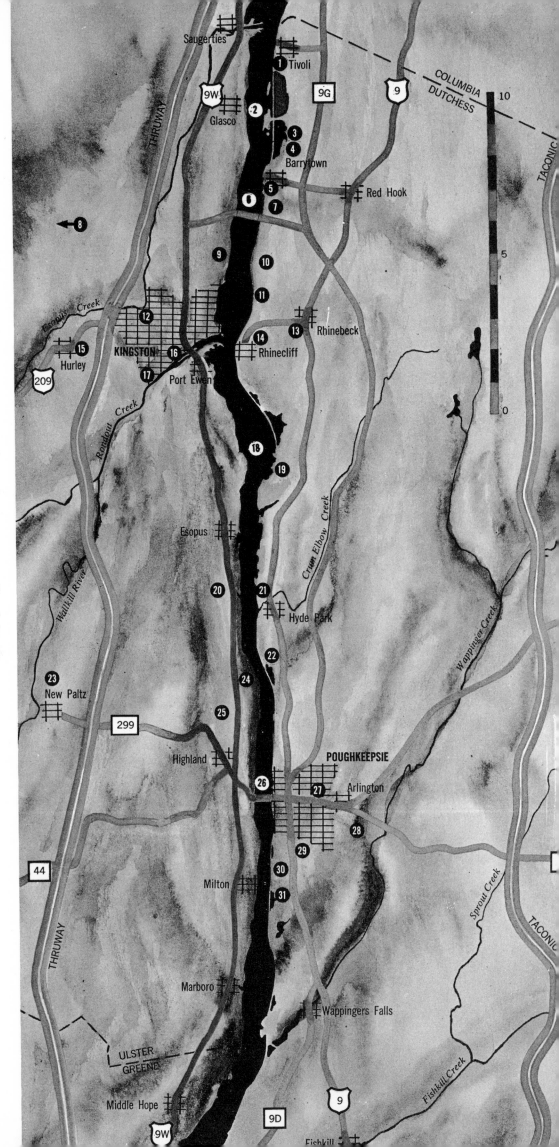

MAP 4:

TIVOLI TO FISHKILL

1. The Pynes, on the site of the Chateau de Tivoli, and *Callender House*
2. *Cruger's Island*
3. *Bard College*
4. *Montgomery Place*
5. *Two octagonal houses and Edgewater,* 1820, Gore Vidal
6. *Kingston-Rhinecliff Bridge*
7. Rokeby, J. W. Chanler
8. Woodstock and skiing center
9. Brickyard ruins, Glasco to Kingston
10. Leacote, Douglas Meritt
11. Ferncliff, William Astor
12. *Senate House, 1676*
13. Beekman Arms Inn, 1710, second oldest hotel in the United States
14. Abraham Kip house, 1715
15. A main street of *early 18th-century Dutch houses*
16. Cement caves and kilns
17. *The old dispatch house for the Delaware & Hudson Canal*
18. *Esopus Meadows Lighthouse*
19. *D. Ogden Mills estate*
20. Home of John Burroughs
21. *Vanderbilt Mansion*
22. *Springwood,* F. D. Roosevelt
23. Dutch stone houses built as early as 1705
24. Concentration of religious orders in one-time estates below Kingston
25. *Fruit area* of west shore chiefly in lower Ulster Co.
26. *Mid-Hudson Bridge*
27. Clinton Museum
28. Vassar College
29. *Springside,* Matthew Vassar
30. Treasure Chest Tavern, 1741
31. Locust Grove, S. F. B. Morse

day in the fall one still sees the scene that Cooper's Natty Bumppo described as "all Creation . . . the river in sight for seventy miles under my feet, looking like a curled shaving . . ."

The Catskill Mountain House is perched on the eastern edge of the state park that encloses six hundred thousand acres of the highest parts of the Catskill Mountains. Like Adirondack Park, it contains many towns and resorts although its industries—hoop-making (which was largely carried on by men who lived alone in wilderness huts), the cutting of saplings for hop vines, mining, and tanning—have disappeared. Nearly two thirds of the area are private land. The art colony at Woodstock, just within the park west of Saugerties, has flourished for half a century. The hills supply millions of gallons of water for New York City; miles of it are stored in Ashokan Reservoir, from which it flows to city mains in three days. The waters of Esopus Creek also flow from Ashokan in the same southerly direction, then turn sharply north behind Kingston to join the Hudson and make a little harbor at Saugerties. Since Catskill has its Creek, and Kingston has the large stream called Rondout Creek. it is a tidy distribution that gives Esopus to Saugerties, midway between. Behind these three river towns the sun sets on the sharp edge of the flat-topped Catskills, which reach their greatest heights in their eastern ranges, while across the river the hills may still shine green and gold for another hour.

Kingston, halfway on the long, navigable part of the Hudson, early became an important town and port. Rondout Creek made a fine harbor, as it does today, although few ships and none of the dashing old steamers crowd its wharves as they once did. During the Revolution the capitol moved from New York to White Plains, to Yonkers, to Poughkeepsie, and at last came to Kingston, considered safely distant from the British on the lower Hudson. But when Clinton decided to raid up-river in 1777, the Highland defenses were easily passed and Kingston was burned to the ground except for one house. The nearby town of Hurley, the refuge of many Kingston people at this time, was unharmed and it still has a number of old stone houses complete to the ironwork on doors and shutters. The Senate House, where the government had only recently drawn up the first State Constitution, was rebuilt on its old site and it still stands. After 1828, when the Delaware and Hudson Canal was built to bring coal from the Pennsylvania fields, Kingston joined Albany as a great shipping center where thousands of barges were directed from a Gothic office on the banks of the creek. Kingston today is a rather bustling town of modern façades laid over late-nineteenth-century downtown buildings, and pleasant hilly streets with tall trees and many churches. Fron Steinman's graceful suspension bridge over the creek, the waterfront section of Rondout is a quiet place of tall, angular brick buildings with an occasional modern touch of glistening aluminum spheres or a valve-sprouting oil tanker.

In the middle of its long, remarkably straight run from Albany to the sea, the river becomes deeper. Where before the river flowed over a softly sloping country and was itself perhaps only twenty feet deep, the bluffs that become sharper and closer to the edge of the river plunge on straight down into its waters. The depth of the river now sometimes reaches one hundred feet and is usually forty or fifty to within a few yards of shore. Frequently it is true that as the river narrows it deepens. For example, while ordinarily a half mile to more than a mile in width in this region, it is one hundred forty feet deep where it turns and narrows to little more than a quarter mile off Crum Elbow.

21

On both sides of the river there have been an increasing number of orchards and vineyards, but around Kingston the west shore becomes heavily devoted to raising fruit while it is more rare on the east. From here to Newburgh fruit stands occur regularly along the roads except for a few miles between Dinsmore and Crum Elbow where a variety of institutions now occupies some of the estates of half a century ago. A number of religious organizations, a school, Father Divine's havens, and a school where boys who have been in trouble or were certain to be shortly are exposed to country living, occupy the huge barns, cottages, and houses. The elaborate Paine estate, with its terraces, marbles, and urns with lion's heads, cost millions, but an institution paid only a fraction of its cost not many years later. Below the wooded estates the fruit belt begins again; here are some of the state's best wine grapes and the cask-full cellars of Italian wine makers.

After the first two bridges below Albany, one for trains and one for a super highway connecting the Massachusetts and New York State thruways, four more bridges span the river in the sixty miles to Poughkeepsie. All of them are lofty enough so that a fifteen-thousand ton liner nearly six hundred feet long and with the tip of its mast one hundred twenty feet above the water can sail under them at high tide with room to spare. Ships with superstructures this tall are not common on the Hudson but even heavier tankers that range around six hundred fifty feet in length are.

The intricate pattern of the truss bridge at Catskill against the hills or the flame of trees in October is interesting, but the Mid-Hudson bridge at Poughkeepsie is a masterpiece of grace and engineering. Still one of the largest, the suspension bridge designed by David Steinman has hardly a straight line, yet has the appearance of great strength without undue mass, much like an organic structure such as the slightly curved femur bone. Seen from a small woods at its western end, the towers rise against the buildings of Poughkeepsie, slim and sparkling in the afternoon, while the huge cables soar up from the saddles and dwindle to curving threads. The black trusswork of a railway bridge thrusts past factory chimneys a few yards to the north, a striking contrast in structure. Trains approach this bridge from the west on trestles built through the thick woods; a motorist going up or down the hill toward the automobile bridge may catch a glimpse of a locomotive or bright boxcar apparently gliding through the treetops.

Poughkeepsie is slightly larger than Kingston, and the river here, being a straight shaft of water between uninterrupted bluffs, is without a harbor. Like Kingston, however, it has its lower, waterfront town where the smallest homes and largest industries contend for space and a few small-boat clubs fly their pennants. The regatta is held here each year, and Poughkeepsie is at present as far north as the Hudson River Day Line's excursion boats venture. The upper town has a compact concentration of stores around two or three main streets, and a typical mixture of houses of an upstate town borders the tree-lined blocks to the country. Southeast of the town the Gothic or extremely modern buildings of Vassar are smothered in their campus foliage. Nearer the river, the Matthew Vassar house still stands; it is a private home in the midst of a large estate, but a gatehouse that still has most of the trimmings of the architectural mode known as Hudson River Bracketed stands virtually at the east curb of the highway leading south along the river from Poughkeepsie.

The soft hills of Dutchess County surround Poughkeepsie, rising higher in the east toward Connecticut and toward Putnam County on the south. Wappinger, Fishkill, and lesser creeks flow down to the river and here again is an area once known for its mills. A hundred years ago, in fact, Dutchess County produced more woolen goods than any other in the state.

South of Poughkeepsie, Wappingers Falls lies deep in the Creek valley, a handsome small town with a widening, wooded inlet that is an excellent anchorage for small craft.

From below Catskill the river has run almost as straight as a canal in a few narrowing reaches of fifteen or twenty miles each. Now it turns southwest around the power plant at Danskammer Point, where Hudson saw Indians dancing on the flat rock, and begins to widen until it becomes one and a half miles across among increasing hills, one of the most delightful areas in its career. On the west bank the last of the fruit farms that have patterned the hills give way above Newburgh to a long suburb of old and very modern houses, some of them extremely handsome.

The two-hundred-fifty-year-old town at the river's edge justifies the opinion that here would be "a very pleasant place to build a Town on," a thought expressed in 1609 by Robert Juet, of the *Half Moon*. Just one hundred years later Newburgh was founded by a small band of Palatinate Germans, refugees from war and famine, who were sent to the new colony under the protection of Queen Anne. Some twenty-five hundred more followed in the largest immigration yet to arrive in the colony, but these were settled up-river where they failed in their attempts to repay the cost of their passage by making tar for the Royal Navy. Newburgh prospered, becoming one of the shipbuilding and whaling towns of the river. It was the headquarters of Washington's forces at several different times, nearby Temple Hill being the place where the restless army encamped after Yorktown while the war they had won occupied the diplomats in Europe for two more years. Generals Knox, Greene, and Gates occupied the handsome Ellison house southwest of town, while Washington's headquarters—where he was offered and coldly refused the crown—were in Jonathan Hasbrouck's house in Newburgh, with a clear view of the signal fires atop Mount Beacon across the river. The Marquis de Lafayette was at the Brewster house south of town on Murderer's Creek, where links for the chain barricade across the Hudson were forged. George Clinton, lawyer, general, and first governor of the state, lived on a farm just south of Newburgh, and Andrew Jackson Downing, who taught the nineteenth-century elite exactly how they must go about becoming gentle, aesthetic, nature-loving, and, in short, civilized, grew up on a nearby farm and learned much himself at the granite and black walnut Armstrong mansion at Danskammer. Responsible for the popularity of the rustic and romantic—along with the Hudson River painters—Downing's own nearby home embodied the principles of landscaping and architecture that he advocated so successfully.

Along the first streets paralleling the river in Newburgh stand many freshly painted, fine houses from its various prosperous periods. Some of the streets leading down the steep hill to the river are ninety feet wide; below on the mile-wide water some of the last ferries on the Hudson sidle along their indirect, cross-current runs to and from Beacon.

Once suffering under the name of Fishkill Landing, the town looking across to Newburgh is now named for its green, conical Mount Beacon, where cable cars clamber up to an observation house sixteen hundred feet above the river. The hills on this side of the river are the first of the Highlands of the Hudson, the narrow spine running closest to the ocean of any of the Appalachians. The river flows on three miles past Mount Beacon until the axis of beetling Storm King Mountain suddenly thrusts eastward and forces the river between its mass and the equally rocky, equally steep Breakneck Mountain.

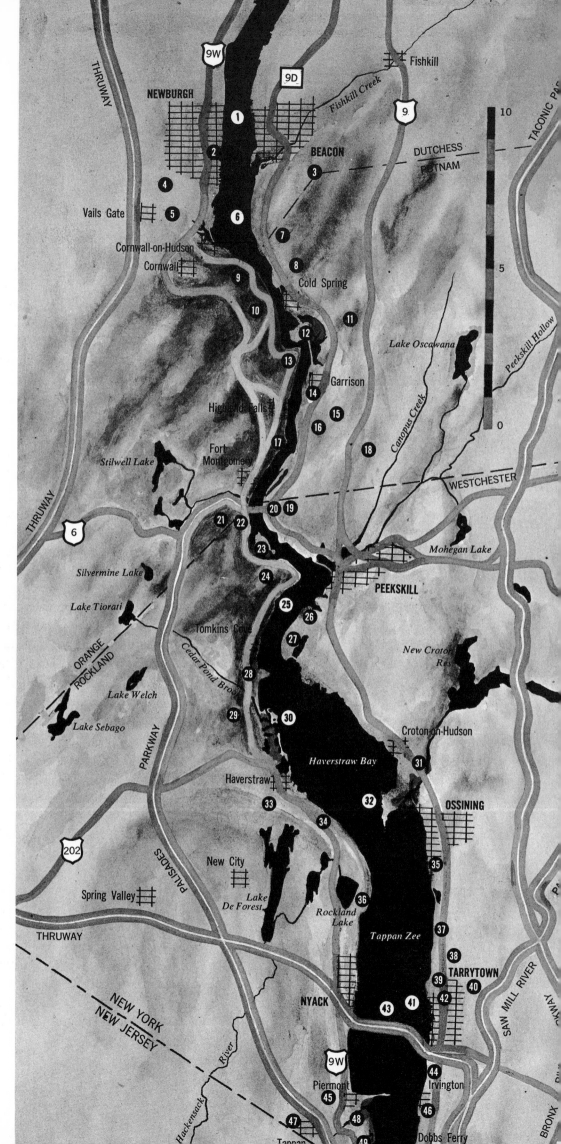

MAP 5:

BEACON TO
DOBBS FERRY

1. *Beacon-Newburgh Ferry*
2. *Washington's headquarters*
3. Mt. Beacon, 1,602'
4. Temple Hill, campsite of the American army, 1781-83
5. *Knox's headquarters*
6. *Bannerman's Island*
7. *Breakneck Mountain, 1,196'*
8. *Bull Hill, 1,425'*
9. *Storm King Mountain, 1,355'*
10. *Crow's Nest Mountain, 1,403'*
11. *Dick's Castle*
12. Constitution Island
13. *West Point*
14. Mandeville, 1737, housed West Point commanders
15. Castle Rock, W. Osborne
16. Site of Beverly Robinson house, Benedict Arnold
17. Pellwood, Alfred Pell and Cragstone, J. P. Morgan
18. Graymoor
19. Anthony's Nose, 900'
20. *Bear Mountain Bridge*
21. *Bear Mountain, 1,305'*
22. Bear Mountain Inn and Fort Clinton
23. *Iona Island*
24. Dunderberg Mountain, 930'
25. *The mothball fleet*
26. Atomic power plant
27. Verplanck's Point
28. *Stony Point*
29. Treason Hill, site of Joshua Smith's farm
30. Grassy Point, *gypsum plant*
31. *Van Cortlandt Manor*
32. Croton Point
33. *High Tor,* 820', first of the Palisades
34. André's landing place
35. *Sing Sing Prison*
36. Hook Mountain, 730'
37. *Rockwood,* Wm. Rockefeller
38. *Old Dutch Church* and Sleepy Hollow
39. *Philipse Castle,* 1682
40. Boxwood, John D. Rockefeller
41. *Tarrytown lighthouse*
42. Monument marking the site of Major André's capture
43. *Tappan Zee Bridge*
44. *Sunnyside,* W. Irving, and Lyndhurst, Jay Gould
45. John C. Fremont grave
46. *Carl Carmer house*
47. Site of André's execution
48. Taulmans (or Tallman) Hill, *view north over Piermont*
49. Snedens Landing
50. *Washington's headquarters*

The old Storm King Highway leaves the six-lane road south of Newburgh to run through pretty, scattered Cornwall-on-the-Hudson. On the slopes of the mountain behind the town some old houses of the Stillman family perch amid some recent, rather luxurious modern homes all of which share magnificent views straight north up the river between Beacon and Newburgh. The highway climbs into the woods and becomes a narrow shelf on the rocky face of Storm King. From here the castle on Pollepel Island, over near the east shore, is an innocent toy. Frank Bannerman bought Pollepel Island as a place to keep the ninety per cent or so of all the arms captured in the Spanish-American War, which he had acquired. He dredged a rectangular harbor off its shores, surrounded it with low, turreted walls so that boats could tie up at the arsenal, and built a replica of a Scottish castle for a summer home. Still the Bannerman property, guarded against any invasion of its privacy but no longer used as an arms depot, the island lies three hundred yards off shore, its architecture and business giving rise to a thousand stories. Storm King Highway turns high above around the rocky mountain to the south and disappears into the Highlands.

The river has suddenly narrowed to three thousand feet between the mountains, and its bottom, which averaged forty feet in the center of the broad reach above, now plunges down to a depth of eighty. Past Cold Spring it narrows even more and turns sharply around West Point. Between this military stronghold and Constitution Island opposite, which was also fortified during the Revolution, the Hudson reaches a depth of 202 feet. It is running true to form: broad and shallow—for the Hudson—in its straight parts, deep and narrow in its turnings. Off several more mountain points in the next few miles it will flow deep—127 feet at Bear Mountain, 165 feet off Iona Island, 91 feet at Dunderberg—but at this sharp, blind angle called World's End where the river is only 450 yards wide, it is the deepest. For ten more miles the river cuts its way between the mountains. Opposite the fields, guns, statues, scores of Gothic buildings, and hundreds of houses that are West Point, a few old estates, mostly converted to institutions, mingle with smaller but elegant homes around the aptly named town of Garrison. As in a good many of the river towns, an old part of Garrison is down at the shore, with a coal company, a tileyard and brickyard, small asbestos-shingled or wooden houses near the steep-roofed railroad station, and a new marina for the increasing swarms of pleasure boats. Once these waterfront areas were all there might be of a town or landing that really existed to serve the needs of the estates scattered along the hills nearby. Sometimes the town grew early and the waterfront became an integral part of the whole, or occasionally the river town would eclipse the village it had once served. Hudson, for instance, which is much larger now than Claverack, was once a satellite of the village, and bore the name Claverack Landing.

Many of the towns below here will also have a main street of modern stores upon the hill where the suburban population shops, and a lower town that most people enter only because the railway is there, or because they keep their power boats there, or, in some cases, because they work in a factory on the river. Garrison has no commercial center uphill, only homes scattered along the two steep roads leading up to the highway and spreading north and south.

A road of rock, loose and hard, climbs a hill beside Indian Brook to a castle. For seven years a man named Dick poured his money into this potpourri of Mediterranean architecture;

after he had spent two millions, he suffered some heavy losses in business. The castle remains incomplete, partially occupied by a family who let visitors walk through it for a small fee.

Glenclyffe houses silent Capuchin friars, and on a hill in the next range from the river the Franciscans of Graymoor command a view over all the surrounding hills and a narrow glint of the Hudson four miles to the south, and offer hospitality to any who seek it from them. The Beverly Robinson house, near Sugar Loaf Hill in Garrison, was used by the commanders of West Point during the Revolution; late in the nineteenth-century this house where Arnold learned of the capture of André burned to the ground.

On the west, Highland Falls and Fort Montgomery offer hotels and cabins for the visitors to West Point between the military reservation and the northern limits of Bear Mountain and Harriman parks. In the woods between towns rose the river homes of Morgans and Pells. The highway crosses Popolopen Creek, whose valley gave British troops a road of attack against the two forts guarding the river and the huge chain the patriots had placed across it. After Forts Montgomery and Clinton were overwhelmed, the British simply cut this chain and sailed north, firing red-hot shot into rebel houses. Today the handsome Bear Mountain Bridge, built by E. H. Harriman when private enterprise had its fullest meaning, spans the river where it squeezes between Anthony's Nose and Bear Mountain. A road even more sinuous than the Storm King Highway climbs up the rock face of the hills toward Peekskill. On the west, Bear Mountain Park and Harriman Park together make the largest division of the nearly fifty-two thousand acres of Palisades Interstate Park, of which the first is the Storm King section. All on the west of the river, the chain of parks is mostly narrow strips of high shore areas, the longest and narrowest being the lower Palisades opposite Yonkers and New York City. The Bear Mountain and Harriman sections contain about forty-four thousand acres and extend from Fort Montgomery southwest to Tuxedo Park, the resort that Pierre Lorillard built for the few, select rich who met his approval. From Bear Mountain's observation tower the town of Peekskill lies southwest beyond the broad turn at Dunderberg Mountain; to the north are the heart of the Highlands and their further ranges over in Putnam County, while below, Hession Lake lies beside three curling roads and the graceful suspension bridge over the river. The combinations of old wooded rocky hills and the now unquestionably great Hudson provides some of the most magnificent river country in the world. More than thirty lakes, swimming pools, picnic areas, a summer music festival, innumerable trails and good roads, and a pier for the Dayliners contribute to the enjoyment thousands experience each year.

Dunderberg is the last Highland barrier. Less rugged than Storm King but with a greater mass, its ridge also runs east and west, thrusting one and one half miles out from the marshes behind the naval ammunition dump on Iona Island to force the river in a widening arc over against Peekskill. In the last dozen miles as the river turned from the rock face of one hill to the flank of the next it has still not bent far from its southerly course. It is one hundred eighty miles from the decisive southward turn near Hudson Falls to the Statue of Liberty in the upper bay, as the imaginary straight line goes. Yet the farthest the Hudson's shores will ever curve to the west from that line is just seven miles, and that but once, and the east shore of the Tappan Zee is the only place where the river is as much as five miles east of it all the way to the ocean. It would be difficult to find another river of this length that keeps as close to the straight and narrow.

As the river turns around under the thick woods of Dunderberg Mountain, more than one hundred twenty ships in eight ranks lie at anchor, spread out for two miles. This is the moth-ball fleet, mostly victory ships from the Second World War, which are sheltered under the lee of the heights to the north and west. In the early morning the waters of Canopus Creek and Peeks Kill, running cold from the hills to the northeast, flow out into the shallow corner of the river across the way and mist rises in a long tongue, a delta of smoking water. South of Peekskill at Indian Point rises a structure novel to the Hudson, an atomic energy plant. The river narrows once more between high, wooded Stony Point, with its Revolutionary War cannon and grass-gown earthen redoubts, and low, scrubby Verplanck's point, whose famous name means now only a sprawling community that looks almost as raw as the scarred sides of its river-front gravel quarry. King's Ferry was an important river crossing here. Late in the war, the British dashed up-river, took the two points, and fortified them. General Wayne asked General Washington for permission to drive the British out, saying that he would storm hell if Washington would plan the campaign. Washington replied that perhaps they should try Stony Point first. The attack was very successful.

Now the Hudson swells out in a curving sea fifteen miles long and as much as three and one-half miles wide in its northern half, Haverstraw Bay. The hills again press close to the river. On the west, at Haverstraw, they become a curved, narrow blade of rock steeper on the river side but occasionally made even sharper on the landward side where quarries have cut their slopes to vertical cliffs. This is the first part of the narrow, basalt ridge that forced its way upward a hundred fifty million years ago to harden into a palisade. Two more thin segments of the Interstate Park enclose most of the heights as they describe an arc down to Hook Mountain, with the river close against the cliffs outside the quarter circle and four lakes grouped together within.

Croton Point, once a gathering place for Indians, crawls southwest toward these cliffs from the opposite shore, its tip almost exactly in the center of the river. The valley of the Croton River and the bird-filled marshes at its mouth, below the point, break the jumbled heights on the east. This river extends as a series of virtually continuous reservoirs straight across Westchester County almost to Connecticut, and these are fed by forty-odd lakes, reservoirs, and ponds that inundate perhaps a fourth of southeast Putnam County. The river's farthest sources are about one hundred wriggling miles from Croton Point, so that, if its waters were not stored behind so many dams and drawn off into town and city mains, there would be a considerable stream joining the Hudson here.

When Pierre, the third proprietor of the eighty-thousand-acre Van Cortlandt Manor, established his home here at the southwest corner of the property in 1749, he enlarged the stone structure where he had probably stored goods to trade with the Indians on the Point, added porches to it and built a ferryhouse that included a tavern. Van Cortlandts lived here continuously for two centuries and kept most of their family documents intact. As a result, despite alterations and the loss of the barn sites in the adjacent highway grading, it was possible to restore the Dutch estate to its eighteenth-century condition with great exactness. Van Cortlandt Manor, thanks to the interest of the Rockefeller family, is complete with its tavern and separate tavern kitchen, proprietor's office, icehouse, "necessary house," gardens, and the old ferry slip.

MAP 6:

HASTINGS TO THE OCEAN

1. Beginning of unbroken wall of Palisades extending south for fifteen miles
2. Park marking site of Draper observatory
3. Indian Head, highest point of Palisades, 547'
4. *Greystone,* Samuel Tilden
5. *Philipse Manor,* 1682
6. Mt. St. Vincent, *Gothic home of Edwin Forrest*
7. F. Van Cortlandt house, 1748
8. *Henry Hudson monument*
9. The Cloisters
10. New York University
11. Fordham University
12. *George Washington Bridge*
13. Jumel Mansion, 1765
14. *Grant's Tomb and Riverside Church*
15. Columbia University and Barnard College
16. St. John the Divine
17. Intensive *shad fishing*
18. Gracie Mansion, 1799
19. *Hamilton-Burr monument*
20. Lincoln Tunnel
21. Rockefeller Center
22. United Nations
23. *Todd Shipyards* and Stevens Institute
24. Holland Tunnel
25. City Hall, 1803, and St. Paul's Chapel, 1766
26. Paulus Hook
27. *The Battery,* Trinity Church, 1697, and Fraunces Tavern, 1719
28. Navy Yard
29. Brooklyn Bridge and Brooklyn-Battery Tunnel
30. Ellis Island, Bedloe's Island
31. Governors Island
32. Brooklyn Heights
33. Staten Island Ferry
34. The Narrows
35. Fort Hamilton
36. Fort Tompkins
37. Conference House, 1668
38. *Ambrose Channel*
39. Sandy Hook Light
40. Ambrose Lightship

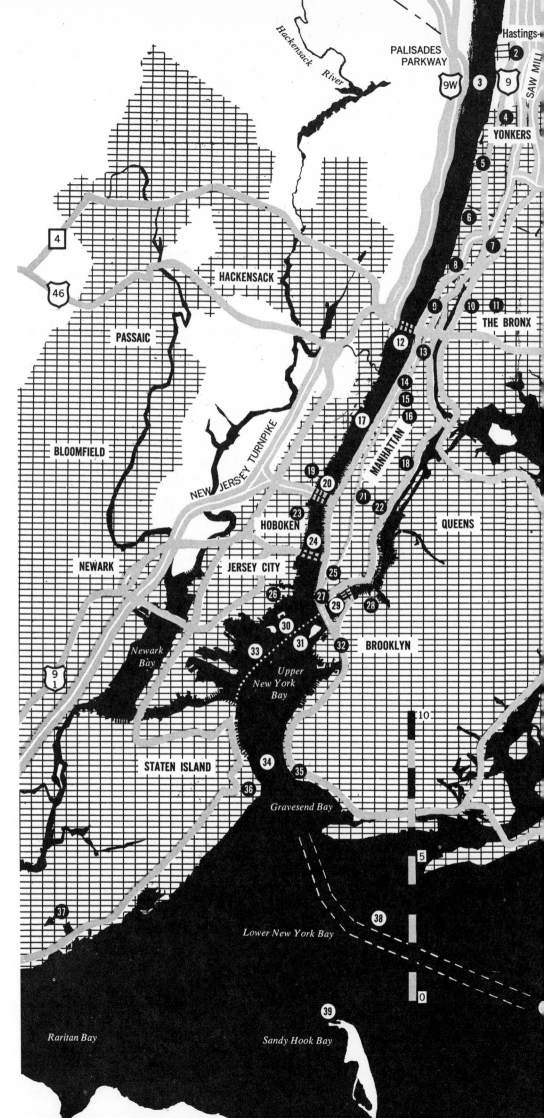

The river traffic increases. Albany is the goal of many of the freighters and tankers swiftly slicing northward, but industry has been mushrooming all along the lower river. Plants at the water's edge have the use of the rails that parallel the river on both sides, the good roads that run sometimes along shore, sometimes a few miles inland, and the convenience of direct shipment at their own piers. Below Poughkeepsie the side-wheeler excursion boats contribute their vintage lines to the scene. And to the barge traffic from the canals in the north are added the long tug-drawn brick or rock-bearing barges from the several brickyards still remaining up-river and the trap rock quarries scattered among the hills on both banks from Beacon to the Tappan Zee. Pleasure craft from kyaks and catboats to fifty-foot yachts seem to be part of a continuing nautical population explosion. The frequent clusters of spherical tanks are fed by large, low-waisted tankers or by smaller square-ended barges looking like oily *Monitors*.

South from Ossining, a town of precipitous streets and a hillside prison, a series of old towns is set among trees above the river. Once surrounded by many estates where today they are more frequently beset with ever-increasing housing projects, these towns still often have handsome centers and beautiful back roads. This is the center of still another great estate that its owner, Frederick Philipse, extended for twenty-two miles, from the Croton River on the north to Spuyten Duyvil on the south and inland to the Bronx River.

Philipse Manor was only half as large as the Van Cortlandt property, which was in turn half as large as the Livingston's, but its owner was known as the Dutch millionaire, the wealthiest man in the colony. Where the Pocantico joins the Hudson north of Tarrytown, Philipse built a manor house in 1682. He was a man of unusual enterprise. A master carpenter, he quickly built mills on the Nepperhan and Pocantico and otherwise cleverly exploited his property, then put his money to work by backing "free trade" enterprises including, it is said, those of Captain Kidd. Through four generations the Philipse family prospered; during the Revolution they remained loyal and their properties were confiscated.

Philipse Castle—so called to distinguish it from the somewhat more stylish town house in Yonkers—has also been restored with the help of the Rockefellers, whose own estate, Rockwood, is just to the north. The old stone house, filled with not just the set pieces but with all the minutiae of an occupied home, and its "new" 1745 addition, with the furniture of its later owners, the Beekmans, are reflected in the millpond among box hedges, willows, ducks, and swans. Along with a wonderfully constructed barn, the mill was restored and functioned for years until the exacting authorities in charge decided that, old as it was, only a restoration of the even earlier original mill would do, and the functioning two hundred-year-old building was dismantled so that an exact replica of the older mill could be built.

Upstream from the millpond, the little Pocantico River flows past the Old Dutch Reform Church and its huge cemetery and under a highway bridge that stands where Irving's famous horseman rose in his stirrups to throw his head after Ichabod Crane. To Washington Irving the Dutch Church where Ichabod sought sanctuary was even then a "monument of bygone days," having been built by Vredryck Flypsen—or Frederick Philipse, as he shortly Anglicized it—and his wife, Katrina Van Cortlandt of Croton, one hundred fifty years before. The modest tombstones of the Dutch settlers march up the hills of the cemetery, changing generations as they go; Irving's grave is in the center of the family plot on a hillside just below the wave of grandiose monuments and somber mausoleums of the latter half of the century.

In Tarrytown the monument to the captors of André also commemorates the period when the Philipse properties made up a large part of the "Neutral Ground," between the British- and American-held territories, which was scourged by cattle raiders and extortionists called cowboys. In a rough way the area north of the British line, which ran somewhere above the towns and manors of southern Westchester, and south of the equally undetermined American line running east from Croton Point, also corresponds to a region favored by the rich of the last century for villa, château, and castle. Following the pattern of other parts of the river, most of these have disappeared or become institutions. This same region again is roughly contiguous with another "neutral ground" of the twentieth-century, the so-called exurbs that lie between the apartments and homes of suburban towns and the limits of reasonably easy commuting. As the distance one may live from the city while still working there has increased, hundreds of thousands have expanded the small towns and changed country and country estates into "exurbia." However, Jay Gould's pinnacled Tudor castle is still the private property of his daughter, Anna, and in neighboring Irvington one of the earliest of country homes, the wildly individualistic Sunnyside, is open to the public. From the porch where Washington Irving often spent an afternoon at work, the broad Tappan Zee is almost the same fine sight it was a hundred years ago, with one huge contemporary structure added.

Between Tarrytown and Nyack a low causeway curves out from the west shore, then runs straight across the shallow water to the Tappan Zee Bridge, swung high above the channel. With its final southward curve over the east shore the bridge and approaches total four miles in length. Here is another place where, if one might stop to look, one might see George Washington Bridge, sixteen miles straight down the river, or catch a glimpse of the Empire State Building on 34th Street, twenty miles away. Looking north past Hook Mountain, one could see the 1100-foot high barriers of the Timp and Dunderberg, sixteen miles over the Tappan Zee.

In the lower part of the river estuary a third flow complicates the pattern of the Hudson currents. Here, where the bed of the river ranges from forty feet below sea level in the wide reaches to as much as two hundred feet in the narrow gorge of the Highlands, colder waters from the ocean floor flow in along the bottom of the river, rise slowly as they become warmer and at last merge in the other currents. This is not a tidal current but a thermal phenomenon that would not be possible were the river shallow or its seaward flow constant and strong.

Two miles south of the Tappan Zee Bridge, Piermont Pier thrusts its length nearly halfway across the river like one of a pair of sliding doors between the broad inland sea and the twenty-four-mile corridor to the harbor. Below the pier a long triangle of marsh, patterned with serpentine streams, is a green or golden-brown carpet at the foot of Tallman Hill. From this elevation, another section of the park jointly administered by New Jersey and New York, one looks down upon the town of Piermont, which, with its hundreds of pleasure boats bobbing off a score of docks, presents a delightful scene, its cluttered and tasteless aspects lost from this distance.

The Palisades melt into hills long enough to accommodate the handsome old and new homes that are Snedens Landing, then recommence, now sheer cliffs rising to five hundred fifty feet that will run south along the river until they dissolve in Jersey City. From the New Jersey line as far as George Washington Bridge, the Palisades are the last section of the park bearing their name. They must appear very like those ramparts first seen by Hudson's men. And indeed, thanks to the heavy growth of trees, much of the east shore north of Manhattan would also seem unchanged despite the hundreds of thousands living within a mile of the river. Tarrytown and Yonkers spread industries along the waterfront, but the small towns between—Irvington, Ardsley-on-Hudson, Dobbs Ferry, Hastings—are revealed only by an occasional small dock, their Victorian railway stations, the spire of a church or an occasional mansion placed to command a view, and, once in a great while, the upper stories of an apartment house. From April until the leaves fall, the hills and towns are mostly concealed under the nubbly mass of green.

Dobbs Ferry was named for Jeremiah Dobbs, a Swedish tenant of Philipse and a fisherman, who offered his boats for a ferry to implement his income. In the late nineteenth-century the townsfolk met to try to find a more distinguished name for the community. The name of Paulding, one of the three captors of André, was on the point of being accepted when a man arose to object against naming the town after such a scoundrel. Rather, he said, name it for another of the trio, Van Wart, who was a gentleman; simply strike off the Dutch "Van" and call the town "Wart-on-Hudson." Dobbs Ferry has come to be accepted.

The other terminal of the ferry that once crossed here was named after Molly Sneden, a Tory who managed the ferry during the Revolution. Her small house stands at the river's edge. The road winds up past the homes of the wealthy little community toward Tappan, where André was taken to be tried and hanged as military law dictated, despite the great respect and love his captors felt for the brave and witty young officer.

The British Navy lay in these waters from 1776 to 1783 and Washington came down to Dobbs Ferry in May of 1783 to meet with Carleton and arrange for the evacuation of British troops from New York. A sloop of war then fired seventeen guns, the first salute by Great Britain to the United States of America.

The grant that at last came to the Yonkheer Adrian Van der Donck a scant two years before his death in 1655 was one of the earliest on the Hudson. Not until Lemuel Wells, who had kept his private domain of Yonkers much as it had been under the rule of the Philipse family, died in 1842 was Yonkers to begin its rapid growth. Today it is the largest city on the river except for its neighbor, which makes it seem small. The second Philipse house stands in a busy center of town surrounded by traffic and industry, and the Nepperhan River, the original source of power for Van der Donck, Philipses, and Yonkers, has disappeared underground.

The city begins to thrust up over the trees more and more insistently. The square, latticed towers of George Washington Bridge carry the high arch of the roadway between the Palisades on the west and the curving wall of apartment houses on the heights of Manhattan. After Inwood and Fort Tryon parks at the northern tip of the island, the stone and brick façades flow south for six miles to 72nd Street, interrupted only by the valley at 125th, man-made cliffs that reflect the sun in the afternoon as do the Palisades in the morning.

Here city streets supplant the landmarks of other times except for a few—the Van Cortlandt house in the city park, Jumel Mansion on the heights above the Harlem River, Fraunces Tavern, Trinity Church, and so forth. The streets of the city have their own story, allied to that of the Hudson but too complex and special to be more than touched upon. Granted that this city would not exist were it not for the river, New York has nevertheless become an independent thing, its enormous population self-generating life and activity; its story is not only too complex to consider but, in many ways, it is too little a part of the Hudson's. The river that formed the city has been influenced almost as much by its huge offspring. It flows on to the sea, an obstacle to be bridged over, tunneled under, used as a port, and blocked out of sight—but still the Hudson.

Below George Washington Bridge on the New Jersey side, apartments and homes atop the narrowing heights between the Hudson and the vast marshes of the Hackensack made a peg-toothed silhouette against the sky. In the narrow strip at the foot of the Palisades, communities lining the single road are a kaleidoscopic jumble of industrial plants, shad fishermen's barges, junk yards of marine and automobile machine parts, clusters of modest to humble homes and boat yards sheltered within the chains of waterlogged barges.

In March the shad arrive at the Hudson. In the lower river the fishermen, often old fellows who have retired from more active deep-sea fishing, plant saplings in the bottom in long rows from the west shore, out of the traffic of the eastern channel. Their nets are hung from the poles so that they float out away from them on the ebb tide and fall back against them when the tide and the shad move up-river. Twice daily, just before the tide turns seaward, the shad men go out in the boats and take the fish, working slowly along the quarter mile or so of net. The shad are quickly sent off to New York or smoked in the fishermen's tiny smokehouses. Farther up-river the shad are caught with nets that are payed out from small boats. The first nets, of course, have the first try at catching the shad, and each net farther up-river will average fewer than those below. Shad were almost fished out of existence but, since the fishing has been regulated, they are increasing again. The only hazard now is the contamination of the river; shad fishermen who have their nets near the mouth of the Hudson jealously guard their rights to these positions, for the less time shad is in the river the better it is.

The west shore line of the railroad, which swung behind the Palisades away from the river at Piermont, now tunnels beneath them and emerges in this narrow area to spread like ivy to shoreside plants, docks, and ferries. Thousands of freight cars lie on the branching lines waiting perhaps to be swung in the slings of enormous machinery aboard railroad ships or perhaps to make their way across river to Manhattan or Brooklyn on barges lashed to both sides of a tug, the whole colorful, busy scene looking from the top of the Palisades like the perfectly scaled toys of the richest kid in the world.

North of the ramps coiling from the mouth of the Lincoln Tunnel where the heights swing back from the river, the monument to Alexander Hamilton stands. The actual scene of the Hamilton-Burr duel—the same site where Hamilton's eldest son had also been killed in an affair of honor three years before—is below somewhere among the rails and roads.

The river has become a port. On both sides docks thrust out from shore, sometimes a thousand feet in length, leaving a narrow half mile of waterway for the tugs, ferries, tankers, naval vessels, barges, liners, junk boats, fishing craft, pile drivers, police boats, fire boats, freighters, excursion boats, dredges, Coast Guard craft, and pleasure yachts that constantly furrow its surface. Busy as it is and surrounded as it is with the enormous expanse of the metropolis, the river still is never dwarfed. The harbor is relieved from the monotony of solid waterfront industry common to many great ports by its backdrops of towering buildings reflecting the sun from myriad windows, by its rocky rampart to the west and its vistas toward the sea or toward the soaring bridges of the East River. Yet forty miles of piers line its complex form.

From the center of the Upper Bay, the inner harbor of the Hudson, may be seen most of the various straits, rivers, islands, and peninsulas that make an interlocking pattern of land and water around this roughly four-mile-square area. To the east the funnel of Gowanus Canal diminishes past scores of piers into a labyrinth of ships and industry deep within Brooklyn. To the northeast Buttermilk Channel runs between low-lying Governor's Island and the wharves beneath the old brownstones on Brooklyn Heights. Beyond, curving around Manhattan, is the East River, which is no river at all but a long, narrow, tide-torn strait between Long Island Sound and the harbor. Almost straight north the Hudson tapers away a dozen miles before it is lost around the corner of the city's structures. Westward the low flat land of Bayonne Peninsula makes a narrow darkness beyond which is the shallow basin of Newark Bay, the Hackensack and Passaic Rivers, and, compact and tiny in the distance, the towers of Newark. Southwest the Kill Van Kull winds past the refineries of Bayonne toward Newark Bay from the ferry docks at St. George, Staten Island, and beyond the last piers on the east of Staten Island and the last in Brooklyn the Narrows flows out between two old forts into the Lower Bay.

The land swims quickly away on each side. The Lower Bay is a more regular body of water than the Upper, far larger and only partly separated from the ocean itself by the six-mile Sandy Hook at the eastern end of New Jersey's Atlantic Highlands. Between the crenelated towers of the Hook and Rockaway Point, six miles of water allow for an ample entrance to the bay. The waters of the Hudson are lost in this immensity; waves breaking upon beaches from Coney Island and Rockaway on the north to Point Comfort on the south are saline and tides are the only apparent movement of the waters. But, following the thin line of buoys along the channel out toward Ambrose Lightship and on out of sight of land, the channel of the older Hudson continues across the ocean floor.

In the ages of ice the oceans were lowered by some hundreds of feet and the larger Hudson, carrying waters from the southern edge of the glacial sheets ran for perhaps one hundred fifty miles beyond the present shore. The force of its waters over thousands of years cut a canyon through what is now again a continental shelf. Starting about fifteen miles from shore as a wide valley some twenty feet deeper than the ocean floor, it sweeps on for ninety miles, deepening until it ends in a delta formation that may indicate one of the ocean's several shore lines. Here, in what they call the Gully, the fishermen of eastern Long Island have discovered that certain fish heretofore presumed to have gone south during the cold months are to be found in profitable quantities.

Finally, a few miles southeast of the delta, begins a great canyon that reaches a depth below the floor of the ocean of two thirds of a mile and with a width of more than five miles. At the continental shelf the canyon again plummets sharply downward to a depth below the surface of a mile and a half and fifteen hundred feet below the ocean floor. Then, one hundred fifty miles from the Narrows, which might ordinarily be considered the river's mouth, the last vestige of the Hudson is lost in the depths of the Atlantic.

October. A spring on Mt. Marcy above Lake Tear.

March. Henderson Lake. Beyond the mountains: John Brown's
farm and grave, Lake Placid, and Saranac.

North from Indian Lake.

National Lead open pit titanium mine and mill, Tahawus.

In the wilderness a few miles from its source,
the first of the Hudson's industries.

Near Riparius.

Lumber, one of the first products of the Adirondacks.

South from The Glen.

Church near Indian Lake.

Warrensburg and the Schroon River.

White house, Indian Lake.

Little gorge at Palmer.

Paper mill, Glens Falls.

In 1872 1,069,000 market logs at least nineteen feet long and thirteen inches in diameter jammed the river at Glens Falls. Lumber that was floated down the Hudson to the mills could be sorted out upon arrival by the brand of the company with which each log was stamped.

Downstream from the dam.

Upstream.

*Pot holes. The rock of the river bed,
carved by the turbulent waters of the falls.*

55

Stables at the track.

Morning among the pines of the Spa.

Saratoga.
The resort, which was fashionable
for more than a century,
is down to its last hotels.

Where Burgoyne's foraging Hessians
were cut down by Stark's men, near Bennington.

*Mill pond, North Bennington. Nineteenth-century mills stand dark
and idle on almost every small stream of the upper valley.*

The British troops that surrendered at Old Saratoga in 1777 were ferried across the Hudson here on the first part of a long march to Cambridge and captivity.

A detail of General Schuyler's home at Schuylerville, burned by the British and rebuilt immediately after Burgoyne's surrender.

The fertile valley. A dairy farm east of Schuylerville.

*A fuel barge in lock No. 5, Barge Canal. Made specifically for the canal,
many barges have only inches to spare on each side in the locks.*

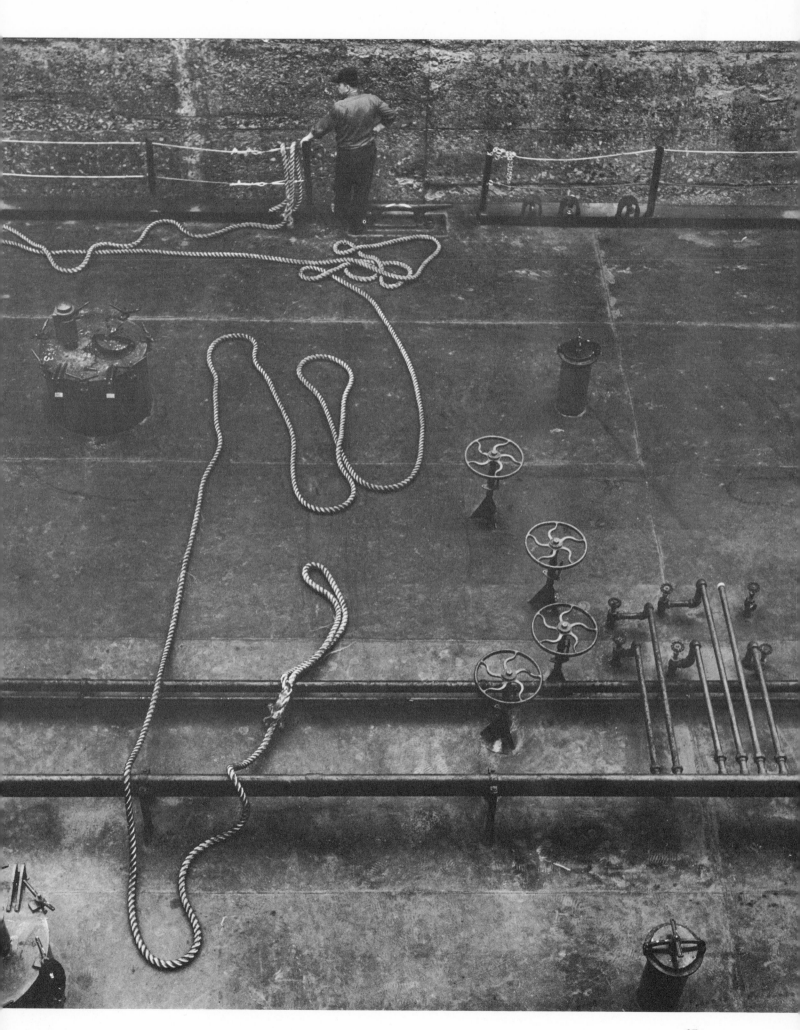

The last six Shakers in a row, graveyard near Albany.
Mother Lee's marker is the slightly taller stone in the right background.

Shaker building, near Albany.

Shaker barns, Mt. Lebanon.

Barn roofs in winter.

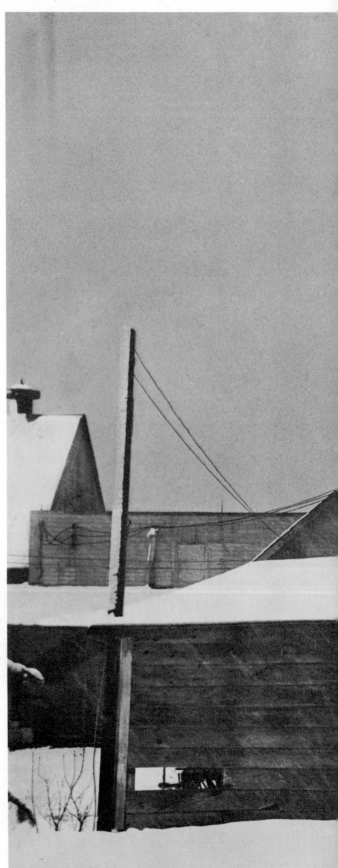

The small town in winter, Burnt Hills.

Schenectady.

Albany's railroads,
where everyone waits,
or changes trains.

Brick drying sheds at the river's edge, near Coeymans.

Cement plant below Albany.

The Hudson valley from east of Clermont.

The House of History, Kinderhook.

Trellised porch, Castleton.

Navigation aid, Nutten Hook.

*Nutten Hook and the town of Coxsackie. One of the last icehouses stands on
the far shore of the river, left, and the chimney thrusting above
the trees on Nutten Hook, center, is part of the ruined powerhouse of another.*

Two old houses north of Hudson.

Ferries, too, have vanished, leaving only their slips and pilings.

Icehouse. The old man said he helped cut the last ice in 1919
at Nutten Hook. The icehouse there was 350 feet by 270 feet.
Burned down. He was a ploughman but he used to cut ice winters.
Good money in it. That last year the ice was
twenty-seven inches thick and it had to be brought down to
twenty-four inches by three shavers so it would fit the
storage space right. But that was the last of it. One by one
the icehouses were torn down or else they burned.
Only two left now and they aren't icehouses. Mushrooms.

The farms and hills of the Taconic uplands, east of the Hudson.

Hudson city, the backs of buildings.

Where whalers docked. Sunset, Hudson.

Dr. Ferguson's house on Mt. Merino.

North from Mt. Merino.
Athens, left, and Hudson City.

92

Church Hill from Catskill.

The Frederick Church house, Olana Castle.

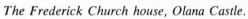

94

Hall and stairs, Olana Castle.

On the following pages, the studio of Frederick Church.

Rip Van Winkle Bridge, Catskill.

Catskill Mountain House.

A New Orleans theater had ordered a number of wooden Corinthian columns from the craftsmen of Catskill. When the theater failed Charles Beach bought the columns. Six went to support the pediment of Christ Church in Catskill and eight stood in a line against the sky on the porch of the Catskill Mountain House.

The town of Catskill, from Christ Church.

Thomas Cole's house in Catskill, from the studio.

Interior detail from Cole's house.

Mills on Esopus Creek, Saugerties.

Esopus meadows light,
the last manned lighthouse on the Hudson.

Farmer's pond at Clermont.

Callender house, Tivoli.

The Donaldson house, one of the largest on the Hudson, is now a part of Bard College.

Author Gore Vidal's 140-year-old home in Barrytown and its view across the river.

The long-lasting artificial ruins of John Cruger.

*Montgomery Place, the home of the young General
who was killed at Quebec early in the Revolution.*

Terrace and view to the river, Montgomery Place.

The Kingston-Rhinecliff Bridge.

A house in Hurley where Washington was given a reception in 1782.

The Steuben house in Hurley, the temporary state capitol in 1777.

The Senate House, Kingston, built in 1676 and burned by the British in 1777.

*Dispatch house on Rondout Creek
that controlled traffic on
the Delaware and Hudson Canal.*

Rondout Creek, Kingston.

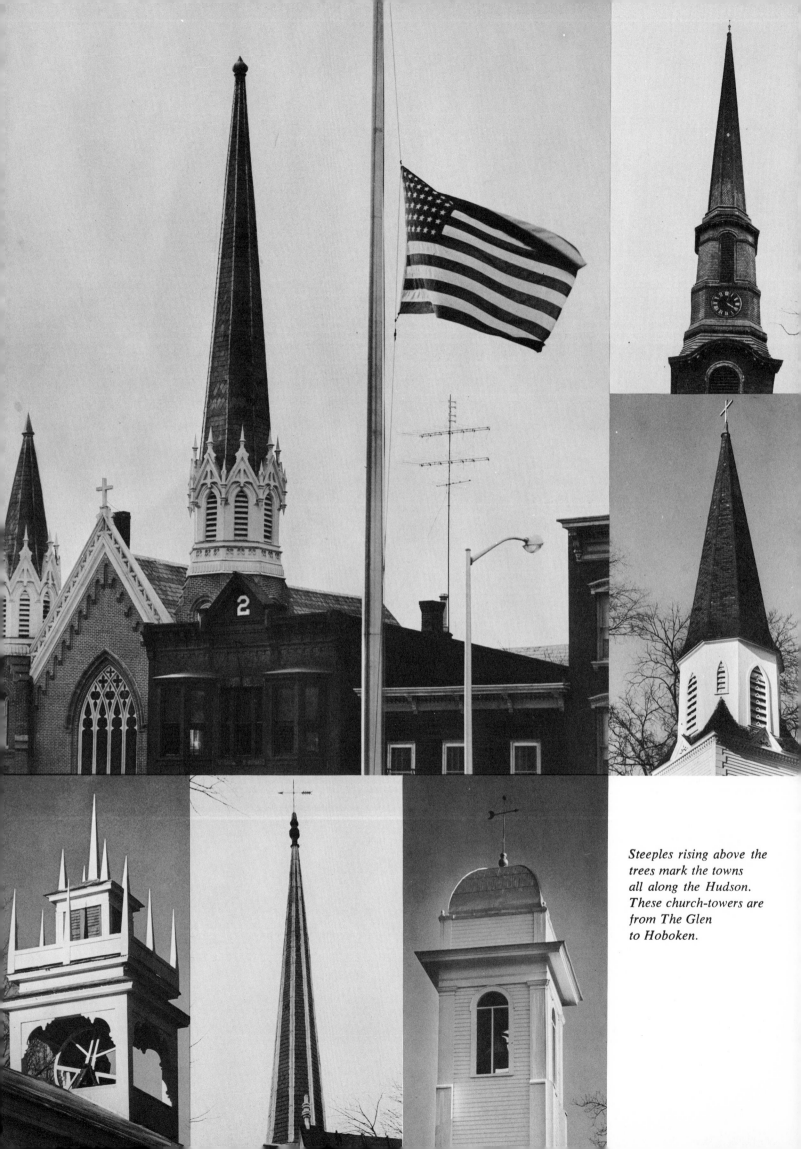

Steeples rising above the trees mark the towns all along the Hudson. These church-towers are from The Glen to Hoboken.

*Antique tubs are less frequent.
The formal facade of the Mills house.*

*A romantic Diana and her hound,
from the Ogden Mills estate.
Lawns and woods of the old houses
often were sprinkled with
statues, sundials,
fountains, gates and temples.*

The Vanderbilt estate from across the river.

*The South portico
of Vanderbilt Mansion.*

West portico, bathroom, and the dark glitter of the gold room.

121

Fruit farms and produce on the west shore.

The Roosevelt house looks out from its bluff to the river.

The Mid-Hudson Bridge in the mist at dawn.

Poughkeepsie and the bridge at night.

Dayliner at Poughkeepsie.

Hudson River Bracketed.
The Matthew Vassar gatehouse, now stripped
of some of its frills, Poughkeepsie.

Newburgh. The old bell tower for the ferry.

Washington's headquarters, Newburgh.

*General Knox headquarters
at Vails Gate, near Newburgh.*

*The broad streets of Newburgh
run straight down to the river
where some of its
last ferry boats shuttle.*

John Stillman's home on Storm King Mountain looks northward up the river.

View from Storm King.
Newburgh, Cornwall, Beacon, and Mt. Beacon.

Living room, Stillman house.

Bannerman's Island at dawn; arsenal and replica Scottish castle.

Bannerman's from Storm King Highway.

South from Storm King.

135

Looking east across the ice-filled Hudson to Bull Hill.

The Ruppert estate, opposite West Point, now a school.

Dick's Castle, interrupted baroque.

North from West Point.
On the left, Crows Nest and Storm King
mountains. The dark mass
at the right is Constitution Island,
fortified during the Revolution.
The narrow reach before it
is called World's End.

The sharp angles of the river between Constitution Island and West Point.

Fortress-like buildings of the Academy.

An officer's residence.

142

Bear Mountain Bridge.

*The road southeast over Anthony's Nose
from Bear Mountain Bridge.*

143

From Bear Mountain to the north.

Palisades Interstate Parkway from Bear Mountain.

Iona Island at night.

*Iona Island, Peekskill and
Dunderberg Mountain from Bear Mountain.*

North to Bear Mountain from Peekskill.

The moth ball fleet, sheltered by Dunderberg.

*Looking across to Stony Point from Verplanck's,
the site of the Revolutionary ferry.*

House at Tomkins Cove.

The lighthouse at Stony Point,
surrounded by ramparts and cannon.

A section of the lighthouse wall,
said to be the stones of the old fort.

The light.

Inside, looking up.

*Spring. Hickory poles ready
for the nets lie at the river
edge below High Tor, Haverstraw.*

*Trap rock conveyors come over the hill
and down to the river, Haverstraw.*

Gypsum plant conveyors, Grassy Point.
At Joshua Smith's farm nearby,
Arnold and André met to
arrange the betrayal of West Point.

Ice on the cliffs.

Buttermilk Falls.

River's edge in February.

Van Cortlandt Manor House, Croton Point.

*The kitchen and tavern at
Van Cortlandt's Croton River ferry.*

158

*Sing Sing. Said to be an Indian phrase
meaning rock upon rock.*

Philipse Castle, Tarrytown.

The gate house of the Rockefeller estate,
Rockwood, near Tarrytown.

162

The office from behind Frederick Philipse' desk.　　*The manor lord's office.*

The dining room.

The Old Dutch Church, Tarrytown.

The Irving family plot.

Sunnyside, that "little old-fashioned
stone mansion, all made up
of gable ends, and as full of angles
and corners as an old cocked hat."

Lighthouse, Tarrytown.

168

The Tappan Zee Bridge.

Leaf-burning at sunset, Tarrytown.

Piermont. Beyond the long arm of land, the Tappan Zee.

Orson Fowler recommended that the octagonal house be equipped with a top studio lighted by a glass cupola; such a room at the top of the house would be perfectly suited for the literary gentleman. Carl Carmer, who has frequently written about the Hudson, has eight sides to his home in Irvington and a light-giving cupola. The unusual dome and decorations of the Carmer house are the ideas of the tea merchant who built it a hundred years ago.

*Octagonal and other multi-walled
buildings of the Hudson.*

*Coxsackie. A thirteen-sided barn
built by Pieter Bronck
supposedly to disprove the
superstitious fears of his slaves.*

Barrytown.

Near Columbiaville.

174

*Sixteen-sided building used
as a gymnasium, Peekskill.*

Hexagonal, Bard College.

Stillwater.

175

North from Hastings toward Piermont and the Tappan Zee Bridge.

A temple pavillion atop an artificial rock hill, Greystone, Yonkers.

A gate at Greystone.

Philipse Manor.

The Palisades near Hook Mountain.

Spuyten Duyvil. Boats heading into the Hudson past the open railway bridge.

Spuyten Duyvil from the Palisades.

*Edwin Forrest's castle became a school,
Mount St. Vincent, where Eugene O'Neill was a pupil.*

Railroads follow both banks of the Hudson.

A time-encrusted retaining wall.

Miles of parks border the river in the city.

Northern Manhattan and the Bronx from the Cloisters.

On the following pages, George Washington Bridge.

Looking north from George Washington Bridge.

In March shad nets string out
toward the city from the
Edgewater flats—
beyond rotting ferry boats,
tugs, scows, and the three ice barges
that have sat in the mud for
fifty years now.
Out of the main channel
along the New Jersey shore
fifty-five rows are set each year.
Twice a day for three months
the men go out along the
sometimes twelve-hundred-foot-long
nets in their twenty-foot
boats to haul in the net
with as many as a thousand bucks
and roes, mend it, and set the
net again for the next tide.

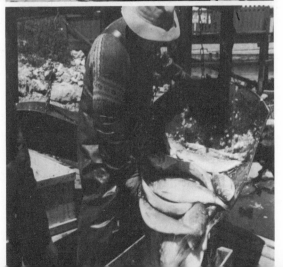

191

*Framed in the signs of an amusement park are Grant's Tomb
and Riverside Church. Where Washington and the new
American Army made their first effective thrust against the
British there now exists a mixed slum of commerce, industry,
and tenements with one viaduct for subway trains and another
for automobiles to pass above this dark depression.*

Riverside Church from the North.

*At sunrise,
the Alexander Hamilton monument in
Weehawken, the Queen Elizabeth,
and the Empire State Building.*

*Row houses in West New York
look across the busy river to the city.*

*Beyond the mile-wide river the gray-green picket fence
of Manhattan glistens in the afternoon.*

Tugboat and ship, lower Manhattan.

Todd shipyards, Hoboken.

198

Two thousand vessels of every kind
enter the busiest port in the world each year.
A few of the ships tied up in
New York harbor on a June day.

From above the approach to Lincoln Tunnel, shipyards, the river, and downtown Manhattan.

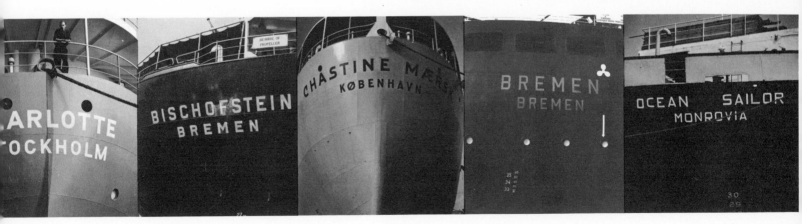

On the following pages, tugboats, East River.

Upper New York Bay from the Battery.

Beyond the Narrows.

Ancient Rome is buried in the mass of centuries of living and in the cauldron of present life. Only tiny vestiges remain to be seen and felt. In Pompeii or Ostia or Herculaneum, buried and preserved, are ruins we can clearly recognize as ancient and Latin.

A river in the Eastern United States is like Rome rather than Pomeii. In the busiest, most vital centers of the New World, history is not allowed to stay among us in concrete form. Houses disappear, and towns change in one or two generations into totally different communities. Entire industries are lost, moved to another place, or are supplanted by new techniques and materials. The whaling industry of Hudson City, for example, has left only a small collection of model ships, harpoons, and scrimshaw in a local museum. Today nothing of the waterfront suggests the colorful atmosphere of a whale-fishing port. Conversely, what were once open fields of battle may now be quartered by scores of city streets. Where American rebels first ran yelling at the heels of beaten British regulars in upper Manhattan a thousand buildings now stand. The historic duel between Hamilton and Burr is commemorated by a monument on the crest of the Palisades in Weehawken, a monument in the midst of a gigantic urban complex that is completely alien to the picture of two gentlemen being rowed over quiet, early-morning waters to engage in an affair of honor.

Still, although there are not streets and farms, castles and churches undamaged for hundreds of years, despite the nearly obliterating growth of the nineteenth century that the twentieth century is scrapping o make way for its even greater profusion, important and colorful events took place along the Hudson, events that influenced the course of all American history.

Before Henry Hudson came, the land had the usual incredibly thin population of Indians. Despite their many names almost all the Indians in the area of the river were Algonquins— Delawares, Mohicans, and Wappingers being the chief subdivisions. Their history ran the placid way of most primitive people: fishing, hunting, occasional raids upon their neighbors, the daily practice of small skills, and the training of the next generation. Along the Mohawk River and west, there were tribes whose fierceness, organization, and encroachments made history. The Iroquois in their Five Nations were feared and known as far north as Hudson's Bay, as far south as Carolina, and as far west as Iowa. They had once walked out to the Mississippi and administered punishment by burning a village. They were the most remarkable people of the North American Indians in their organization; no others, even under the stress of threatened extermination, approached their understanding and ability in this area.

Certainly the Algonquins, their nearest and dearest targets, did not. The Algonquins along the Hudson occasionally resisted the force of the two thousand Iroquois warriors with their larger numbers but they did not have any idea of how to drive them away or placate them permanently. Between crises they continued their calm, unchallenging life beside the River-That-Flows-Two-Ways.

Since Columbus, all the Tudors, from Henry VII to Elizabeth I, had come and gone in England and the Stuarts were ruling before the time of Hudson's voyages. For over a century the New World was ignored by the northern powers except for their attempts to find a way past it to India. The Hudson had been discovered in 1524 by Giovanni da Verrazano, who reported to Francis I of France that he had found a mighty river with a good harbor. He might as well have stayed at home; the time was not right. The dffiiculties inherent in exploration and settlement were large enough and, furthermore, people simply did not want to leave the excitement of the Renaissance for the wilderness. There was little interest in the new land or its possibilities, and there were no investors. The land and the Indians were to have peace for three more generations.

Sailing for the Dutch East Indies Company, Henry Hudson turned away from a third attempt to find an open waterway to India through the Siberian Arctic toward America. From Virginia he sailed north along the coast looking for the transcontinental passage that, it was rumored, existed somewhere in the north. On September 3, 1609, the eighty-ton *Half Moon* entered the outer bay of the Hudson River, a river large enough and deep enough to be the passage they sought. The Indians were curious and friendly and swarmed out to the strange vessel. Hudson went ashore and was guest at a feast where the Indians sang for him and made it seem truly that this was "as pleasant a land as one can tread upon." Yet a few days later First Mate John Coleman was killed by an arrow when the boat in which he and four of the crew had been exploring up the river was suddenly attacked from two canoes. At Yonkers, too, the *Half Moon* was threatened by war canoes but escaped without casualties, and this was important, since not many casualties could be suffered by this group, numbering only about twenty, if any were to survive.

Hudson continued slowly upstream past the vertical wall of rock on the west into a wide sea, through the highlands and beyond, and the river was still salt and still tidal. For almost three weeks the *Half Moon* sailed on, past the mist-filled valleys spilling down from mountains in the west, sounding their way among the islands now growing more numerous as the water became shallower. On the seventeenth Hudson went in a native canoe to the east shore as the guest of a small band of Indians. There he was feted and saw corn and beans drying in the sun—"enough to load three ships." As he left them, the Indians, thinking he withdrew from fear, broke their bows and arrows and showed them as signs of their good feelings. In these upper parts of the river all was apparently congenial and amid frequent crowds of natives they sailed nearly to the site of Albany. A small boat was sent on from there to find whether the water grew deep again, although all but the slightest hope of finding a passage must by now have vanished. When the boat returned at night in the midst of a sudden rainstorm and reported the end of navigable water, their journey was finished.

Dropping down-river somewhat more quickly than they had sailed up, they continued to exchange gifts with the Indians and had no trouble until they were again south of the highlands. Somewhere near Stony Point an Indian who had been loitering out of sight in his canoe under the high stern of the *Half Moon* saw his chance and entered a cabin through the window. Someone saw him leaving with a few odd items he had found irresistible and shot him. All the natives who were aboard to trade leaped overboard, striking out for shore. When a small boat put out to recover the stolen shirts and a pillow that were floating in the water, one of the swimming natives grabbed the gunwale of the boat and tried to capsize it. The cook cut off the man's hand with a sword. From there to Manhattan the ship was followed by parties of Indians in war canoes, bent upon revenge and discharging volleys of arrows. Musket fire kept them off and killed two of a group of about one hundred Indians who were gathered on a point to attack the ship as it passed. This may have been Croton Point, which extends halfway across the wide Tappan Zee and was a traditional place for Indian gatherings and trading.

Finally drawing away from the hostile Indians, they reached the harbor, and by October 4 they were on their way back to Europe. Hudson landed in England, where reports of his discoveries aroused great interest. He was forbidden to return to Holland and was sent out in the spring under the auspices of an English company. That last famous voyage ended with a mutiny in the bay that was also to bear his name, and where he undoubtedly perished with his son and other members of the crew in the small boat in which they were set adrift.

The time was now coming near when the New World would begin to attract people and keep them, rather than simply be a goal for explorers. In 1606 King James had authorized two companies to settle in America. The Plymouth Company was to hold all the land between what is now Eastport, Maine, and Long Island, a slice some three hundred miles wide from north to south. An equal territory, lying between Cape Fear, North Carolina, and the present southern boundary of Delaware, went to the London Company. The two-hundred-mile-wide band between the two companies might be open to either. Neither of these grants was bounded on the west but rolled, presumably, as far as the land went. By these official acts most of what is today the United States was, in English eyes, registered as English territory. Others were not welcome.

In 1607 the English had set up a colony at Jamestown and the Plymouth and Massachusetts colonies were founded in 1620. But in the meantime the Dutch had followed up the explorations of Hudson by sending ships to investigate further his river and to make preparations for settlement of this fertile land. In 1614 their ships returned to Holland with maps of the area, leaving a fort near Albany. Despite the favorable reports the prosperous Dutch delayed until 1624 before returning, and then their settlers were mostly Walloons fleeing from Spanish repression. With eighteen families in Fort Orange (Albany) and eight men on Manhattan the Dutch began the European settlement of the river. They had correctly chosen to occupy the two strategic sites that could control the life of the river.

Still the new project progressed very slowly. The small numbers who came were more interested in trading for furs with the Indians than in farming. The Dutch West Indies Company saw clearly that without the stability of a permanent and self-sustaining population their company would not be profitable nor would their claims endure. The English, the French, and the Swedes were all colonizing within a few hundred miles.

In 1629 the company decided to accept a plan that one of their directors, the diamond merchant named Kiliaen Van Rensselaer, had suggested. They offered large blocks of land to those who would guarantee to develop them and establish fifty permanent residents on each. Six of these patroonships were granted, although only that of Van Rensselaer lasted. These company grants, which were permanent fiefs of inheritance and carried with them duties and privileges very like those of feudal lords, resembled other charters and grants that were also frequently bestowed by the English in the New World. However, the large land holdings of the Hudson River valley were to be unique in America.

In all the northern colonies there were relatively few slaves or indentured servants; the Pilgrims and Puritan English as well as the self-reliant Dutch rejected the idea of slavery, and most of the settlers in the north were not people of sufficient means to own slaves in any case. But with the large grants came many of the same problems that beset southern estate owners; who was to work the land? A largely feudal system became the pattern on the patroon's holdings. The lord of the manor set up stores, mills, and docks; he provided the land; he established courts. His tenants worked the land, paid him in kind, and abided by virtually any of his decisions upon penalty of prison or dispossession. The farmers on these grants along the river could not actually own the land nor could they transfer it without consent and fees. Some of those landowners who opted for the patriot side in the Revolution were able to continue this system, largely unmodified, until the middle of the nineteenth-century. The lordly owners had enormous power in both colony and state and the abolition of various loyalist grants during the Revolution may have given a certain measure of satisfaction to the rebellious common people even though, as it turned out, these lands rarely became available to them.

In 1664 the British looked to their charters and found that New Netherlands, a town in the center of their seaboard that was more and more taking their colonial trade to Holland in Dutch bottoms, was also occupying Plymouth Company territory. Assembling a small fleet and a small army—but enough to outnumber the usual tiny Dutch garrison—they came to New Amsterdam and took it without a shot. It was one of the most pleasant transfers of power the world has ever seen. Aside from having to learn some English in order to transact official business, the Dutch could go about their affairs much as they had.

They had lived in peace with their English neighbors and now they continued to live in peace as a part of England's possessions. One way or another the Dutch became English. Van Rensselaer's widow soon married the young and acquisitive English clerk Robert Livingston. Vredryck Flypsen became Frederick Philipse and sent his sons to England for their education. Peter Stuyvesant and the new governor, Richard Nicolls, became good friends and city neighbors. The shrewd and energetic burghers made their power felt within the community.

This brief period from 1613, when the first fort was raised at Albany, to 1664 was the entire span of Dutch control of the Hudson except for about one year when the Dutch took New York again in the course of a dispute with England, then once more returned it. But the advantage of being first is apparent in the Hudson River country, for, despite their small numbers and short tenure, Dutch names are sprinkled everywhere—though frequently in English distortions—from Hoboken, Spuyten Duyvil, the Bronx and Yonkers to Catskill, Rensellaer and Watervliet, and the scores of streams called "kills" that flow into the Hudson. Dutch family names such as Rensselaer, Stuyvesant, Vanderbilt, Verplanck, Roosevelt, Van Cortlandt, Schuyler have been prominent in the history of the valley from the beginning until today.

For the next century the British and French struggled for supremacy in North America. The Hudson River was of paramount importance in this struggle. In a period when water provided by far the most efficient means of transportation the rivers were the arteries along which settlements naturally grew. They were also the means by which armies could move rapidly. The thin, glittering blade of the almost continuous waterways of the Hudson, Lake George, Lake Champlain, and the Richelieu River was a double-pointed dagger impartially offering a highway for attack in either direction. The French, having taken precedence over the British in the north, where their towns and fortifications were spread in a great arc along the St. Lawrence and Lakes Ontario and Erie, feared an attack upon Montreal and Quebec. The English were equally concerned that the French might sweep south to cut their seaboard in two. Both nations extended their areas of control, built fortifications, and enlisted the aid of Iroquois and Algonquins as the struggle over their conflicting claims became imminent.

In the colonial aspects of the four wars between Britain and France the Hudson River was repeatedly threatened and attacked. In the first of these desultory wars two hundred French and Indians utterly destroyed Schenectady, scattered the Iroquois in the Mohawk Valley, and, but for the efforts of Peter Schuyler, probably would have succeeded in making a separate peace with them and might even have turned them against the British. The second war by-passed the people and territory of the Hudson River (although it was ultimately of importance to them that France lost a great deal of Eastern Canada as a result), and the third outbreak of hostilities was a kind of variation on the first: Saratoga was burned this time and it was William Johnson who kept the confidence of the Iroquois in the face of widespread French victories.

Nothing was settled by these three wars. In sixty years the French, trying desperately to cut off English influence and expansion in the west, had extended their loosely held area into the Ohio River country to link their Canadian and New York territories with those in Louisiana. The British in the same period had vastly increased in numbers along the Atlantic coast but had now to face the necessity of a much greater effort in order to make New York safe against attack. It seemed quite possible, in the light of the fairly even struggle that had occupied the last sixty years, that the French might be able to gain control of the Hudson despite the fact that in America they numbered only about 80,000 while the British population was more than 1,100,000. This 14-to-1 ratio was not the favorable factor it might have been in a war of attrition or an Indian-style war, which used the local militia. The wars in America were fought primarily with regular troops from the homeland, especially by the British, and the primary targets were the cities and strongholds. Indian allies and local populations were factors of importance, as were fortified posts, good harbors, and food supplies, but European generals considered the trained army unit to be the key to victory anywhere; the idea of placing reliance upon a militia of farmers and merchants was senseless. In any case, the farmers and merchants agreed. The various English colonies were loath to co-operate in a common effort against the French. In the first war with the French, when the main attacks were made against New York, moneys for defense could not be obtained in sufficient amounts even from the New York Assembly. It was up to the English.

For the fourth phase of the struggle, therefore, the English decided to increase their efforts in America and at least gain from this long series of conflicts a decisive preponderance of power. Again, very little of this French and Indian war took place along the Hudson River. After several victories from Ohio to upstate New York, the French were in more solid control of the northern and western parts of New York than they had been three and one-half wars ago.

Still more British troops were sent and French ports were blockaded. After a second effort to take Ticonderoga failed, the tide turned. Quickly the French were forced out of Frontenac on Lake Erie, and they abandoned Fort Duquesne on the Ohio. Amherst took both Ticonderoga and Crown Point, while Wolfe's army won a brilliant victory at Quebec and William Johnson's Indians helped take Fort Niagara. The long struggle ended. The French relinquished their claims to all Canada and to everything east of the Mississippi except New Orleans. Only Spain and England remained in North America, and their areas of settlement and exploitation were remote from each other. The colonies, and particularly the colony on the Hudson River, were now free of threats against their future welfare and growth.

The mother country felt, and reasonably enough, that the colonies should share some of the great cost of the wars that had made them secure. The Americans had not co-operated with each other, had contributed very little money, and were now refusing to help as the British found themselves again at war in 1763. This time the trouble began with the Indians west of the Alleghenies, who feared that the unleashed colonies to the east were certain to take all their lands. Heavily in debt, and with defense costs that were now annually eighteen times greater than they had been before, Great Britain introduced taxes to be levied directly on the colonies and at the same time, in an attempt to secure peace in the west, prohibited land grants to white men west of the mountains and allowed trade with the Indians only by license.

Here was laid the train leading to the explosion of the Revolution. Taxation of itself was not the cause of dissension; a principle and a practice were involved. During the last century the colonists had gradually gained for themselves a series of rights, or what they considered to be rights by virtue of long practice. The colonial assemblies had become centers of increasing self-government ever since they had been formed. The New York Assembly had first been called in 1683 when James, Duke of York, decided to allow the colony to become self-governing. A charter for this purpose was drawn up and the Assembly also passed several laws, but James, becoming King, revised his ideas and withheld approval of the charter. The Assembly persisted. Its influence was considerable in that the costs of government in the colonies were met by taxes decided upon and raised by order of the Assembly in Albany, which thus developed a weapon of the greatest effectiveness against any unpopular act of the King's governors in the colony.

Besides the exercise of self-government in the assemblies and other governmental procedures, the colonies had developed toward certain political freedoms that presaged the American climate of liberty. James II attempted to weld the colonies into more effective military units in the struggle with France by appointing Sir Edmund Andros as single governor over all New England, New York, and New Jersey in 1688. Sir Edmund stayed briefly in New York, abolished the Assembly, and then went to Boston, where he also abolished the Assembly, took the powers of taxation unto himself and otherwise curtailed that colony's privileges. Unfortunately for Sir Edmund, James was then fleeing to the continent before the might of William of Holland; Boston jailed Andros and restored its former government, while New York took advantage of the news from England to stage a little revolution. Jacob Leisler, a German merchant who had lived in New York since just before the British took it, found considerable support among small tradesmen and laborers for his opinion that since William III was now King the officials appointed under James should be ousted. This included not only Sir Edmund's deputy but the council of prominent citizens, such as Frederick Philipse, Nicholas Bayard, and Stephen Van Cortlandt, that he had appointed to help govern the colony. With small revolts flaring in the counties around the city, Leisler's faction turned out these appointees and Leisler declared himself lieutenant-governor of New York. Albany refused to recognize Leisler but after he sent men north to help against the French, who were raiding uncomfortably close in the first year of war, burning nearby Schenectady in February 1690, they were more tolerant of the New Yorker. Leisler next called for a Congress of American Colonies to draw up plans for an attack upon Canada. Representatives of New York, Massachusetts, Plymouth, and Connecticut met in New York, and Rhode Island and Maryland pledged their aid.

After this year of "independence" King William's newly appointed Lieutenant Governor Richard Ingoldsby arrived in New York and Philipse, Bayard, and Van Cortlandt were again appointed members of the council. Leisler refused to surrender the fort to Ingoldsby and after weeks of indecisive waiting, orders, counterorders, and the mutual ignoring of orders, Leisler's troops fired on those of Ingoldsby as they marched too close to the fort. On the next day the Governor, Colonel Henry Sloughter, arrived. Leisler was now not only less popular than he had been at the beginning of this revolt, but he must be considered a treasonous rebel if he further resisted. His position was hopeless and he surrendered. Condemned to hang, before his execution he expressed the hope that all malice and hatred aroused by recent events might die with him.

However, certain divisions had been exposed in this revolt that were to persist into the revolutionary period some eighty-five years later. The farmers, laborers, and small businessmen who mistrusted the wealthy merchants, lawyers, and large landholders and threw their efforts behind Leisler were the same groups that provided the popular support for the more radical elements before and during the Revolution. Although many of the influential men of the colony would become leaders of revolutionary sentiment, there would be a great many others who would remain loyal to the King's government, in which they had so long held important positions. Even more would be concerned in desperate efforts to modify the more extreme trends of the Revolution, fearing the popular rule more than any other form of government.

While the power of the Assembly in New York was re-established and the members were elected by the citizens—which meant, at this time, ten or twelve per cent of the population—the governor was also a man of considerable power, and an appointee, who varied in tact, ability, and effectiveness. In 1734 the then Governor Cosby was annoyed at certain criticisms of his policies that were published in the *Weekly Journal,* a paper less than a year old. Its publisher was John Peter Zenger, who had arrived in America at the age of thirteen in the wave of Palatinate refugees who were settled in seven communities up-river on Livingston land and across the river on the west bank. Required to make tar to pay for their passage and settlement before they might become independent landholders, the Germans faced a series of insuperable difficulties. After two years the funds for their support ran out, and when they were facing starvation they were told they would have to make their way on their own. Some managed to reach the Schoharie valley, some returned to New York City, some became tenants of Robert Livingston and others spread out elsewhere along the Hudson. Rhinebeck is a nostalgically named town of the Palatinate Germans.

Young John Zenger came to New York and was apprenticed to a printer. His articles about the ills of his time were denied publication in the cautious press. With funds from political critics of the governor, Zenger set up his own paper, in which it was promptly asserted that courts had been established without the consent of the Assembly, that the governor removed judges without cause, and that voting privileges were denied men who had the right to vote. Zenger was brought to trial for libel. The contest was uneven, with the services of the leading New York attorneys denied him and a judge whose sympathies were clearly not disposed in his favor. But the jury agreed that Zenger was not guilty of printing false statements. Since this became the definition of libel, it was a decision of considerable significance and a specific illustration of the advance of freedom in the colony of New York.

While British troops were still occupied with campaigns against the Indians and the Crown was busied with its efforts to reduce the impertinent autonomy its American subjects apparently felt they had achieved, the great landholders were suddenly faced with their own rebellion. Certain of their tenants, of whom some were always a source of trouble, had risen in protest against the seizure and imprisonment in New York of two farmers for non-payment of rent. William Prendergast, a tenant of Frederick Philipse, rose to the leadership of an army of tenant farmers and threatened to march on the city and release the prisoners. From a few hundred the army swelled to thousands as it moved south from Dutchess County.

The rebellion enlarged its aims. The rents, which had been paid yearly for a century and more and which amounted to many times the value of the land, which could not be bought, must now be abolished. If this made the farmers communist "Levelers" like the extremists who had risen to make similar demands during the Commonwealth in the home country, so be it: they were "Levelers." Prendergast happened to pay an annual rent that was the same amount paid to the Crown by his landlord for all of the Philipse property. The rights of those to whom the land had been granted so long before were reinforced by the law, but the law must now be changed since it was unjust.

The mob thrashed judges, put dispossessed tenants back on their farms, and marched down toward a terrified city. Learning of the concentration of troops awaiting there, Prendergast decided against an attack on Fort George and the city and turned back up-river to harry the Livingstons, Philipses, Schuylers, and Van Cortlandts, emptying jails and threatening sheriffs. The landlords sent desperate appeals to the governor and at last three hundred regulars landed at Poughkeepsie with orders to take William Prendergast. Disregarding diversions by his followers farther north, the British troops followed the rebel leader relentlessly. The troops were approaching a house where Prendergast had gone to earth when some of his militia fired upon them from surrounding fields in circumstances much like those to be repeated with graver effects in Massachusetts nine years later. The disciplined soldiers pressed on to their objective to take fifty prisoners, but William Prendergast was not among them. Shortly persuaded by his Quaker wife to give himself up, William and Mehitabel rode into the redcoat camp together.

After a month's imprisonment in New York, Prendergast was brought back to Poughkeepsie to stand trial for high treason. Mehitabel was a wonder of brave resourcefulness in her husband's defense. Her unflagging efforts to mitigate his crimes led the prosecution to demand that she be removed, but young Judge Robert Livingston, despite being one of the most prominent of the class attacked by Prendergast, not only allowed Mehitabel to remain and continue her efforts but even refused to accept the first verdict of guilt from the jury. When the jury returned with the same verdict a second time, Judge Livingston, under the law, had to condemn the prisoner to hang.

The trial had taken twenty-four consecutive, sleepless hours, but Mehitabel, realizing the inevitable outcome and the likelihood of mob action to free her husband, immediately set off on horseback for New York to seek a pardon from the governor. In three more days she was back, having ridden one hundred eighty miles and persuaded Governor Moore to send a petition for royal pardon (which she composed) to the King and to grant a stay of execution until an answer should be received. Prendergast dissuaded his followers from their plan to free him and six months later King George pardoned William Prendergast in the hope, he said, that his clemency might have a better effect than punishment.

The uprising subsided. Thousands of its partisans would have their hopes raised again during the great rebellion just ahead, but they would again fail to achieve their personal and economic independence from the lords of the manors.

As the British Government, obviously underestimating the degree to which freedom had become a cherished part of the American life, prepared to enforce the collection of the new taxes, the New York Assembly hastened to frame a protest, stating that they had long enjoyed the right to tax themselves and that the abrogation of this tradition would destroy the liberty and security of the people. This had no discernible effect in Parliament, and Committees of Correspondence, created in the various colonies, were to co-operate in opposing the new policies in whatever ways they could. During this time the people of New York split into two main factions, one of which was Tory, Episcopal, and mostly made up of rich merchants and landowners of the lower river and New York City, such as Delancey, Van Cortlandt, De Peyster, and John Cruger. The other party was Liberal, Non-conformist, and mostly led by up-river landed gentry and city lawyers such as William Livingston, Isaac Sears, and John Scott. New York had become the military center of the British Army in America and the numbers of troops in the city created more than the usual amount of fears and tensions. However, one contest—the continual erection of liberty poles by the newly formed Sons of Liberty and the equally persistent efforts by British troops to cut them down—went on for months with remarkably little serious trouble.

The more radical element gained strength in the Assembly as it became apparent that the British were not going to be dissuaded from their program. The protests being sent to Parliament became so strong that the governor dissolved the Assembly. An all-colony boycott of British goods resulted in the repeal of all new taxes except for a token tax on tea, by which England indicated that she reserved the right to tax the colonies directly despite their protests. Tensions were eased for a time, and the colonies evaded this issue by smuggling tea from Holland.

William Tryon, a man considered by New Yorkers to be a reasonable, just, and charming person, became governor in 1770 and immediately set about to do whatever he could to improve matters. Other than continually urging moderation on both sides and employing all his persuasive skill, Tryon could do little; he was a loyal appointee of his King and a sympathetic resident in America and he was unable to direct policies or emotions on either side of the Atlantic. In 1773 Parliament rescinded all duties on tea, retaining only the very small American tax. At the same time, however, the tea trade was made a monopoly of the East India Company. The affront of this effort to tempt Americans into paying taxes and at the same time quit smuggling their tea resulted in reactivated Committees of Correspondence, the Boston Tea Party, and a similar occurrence in New York harbor (although without the Indian regalia), and the judicious return to England of one ship whose captain made no attempt to land his tea.

Many conservatives now found it necessary to join with the more radical elements in order to keep revolutionary fervor in check. The Committee of Correspondence in New York was enlarged and, as British repressive acts continued in Boston, it found either that it had to be the vanguard of anti-ministry efforts as a whole or that the radical minority would take over. The Committee called for a Continental Congress and named five moderate delegates to attend, all of whom were endorsed by the voters. In Philadelphia the Congress resolved to boycott British and West Indies goods. In New York the Committee of Correspondence again increased its membership and again became more radical. The Assembly in Albany remained conservative and began to find itself ignored as a governing body. When in 1775 it refused to name delegates to the Second Congress, the Committees again selected them.

There had now arrived a time of decision. Independence was still not an aim, nor even considered desirable by most responsible people, but the possibility of conflict could not be ignored, and implicit in this possibility was that of independence. If the only way in which the colonies should be able to resist paying taxes levied directly upon them, if the only way to preserve their liberties were to oppose the British troops and excise officials with force, then they would most likely be considered rebels against the King. They would then be engaged in a struggle for independence as an integral part of their struggle for justice. But no one wanted this. In the papers of the most extreme radicals of the time the word "liberty" is the one found on almost every page, not "independence."

When the news of Lexington was brought to New York in April 1775, the radicals took power and New York became an apparently revolutionary town. Despite the concentration of the King's troops and arms in the city alongside an increasing number of militia, there were still no clashes between them. When arms were seized and royal magazines raided, the Provincial Congress did all it could to recover the stolen weapons. There was no war with Britain despite the blockaded harbor at Boston, despite Ethan Allen's capture of Ticonderoga and Crown Point, and despite all the preparations being frantically hastened for battle and defense. British warships lay in New York Harbor, having taken the city garrison aboard, but they were being supplied by order of the Provincial Congress! Tryon returned from England, where he had been on leave, just in time to go unnoticed in the midst of the festivities for George Washington, who was en route to Cambridge to assume command of the American forces there. At last, as must happen in such situations, a panicky shot fired by some American toward a small British boat provoked the British into a short bombardment of the city. Perhaps a third of the citizens immediately left town, some in fear of the British and some, who were either Tory or not radical enough for their neighbors, in fear of the Americans. Other Tories remained but were now beginning to be arrested and sent to Connecticut, where it was thought they would be able to do less damage. Governor Tryon gave up hope of bettering the situation and went out to the warships *Asia* and *Kingfisher*. Troops from New York had gone north in August to help in the attack on Montreal and Quebec under Schuyler, Montgomery, and Arnold.

At the end of 1775 the Americans had lost the battle of Quebec. Young General Montgomery had been killed, General Arnold wounded, and the entire attempt to convert Canada to an ally had backfired at enormous cost in lives. Thirty thousand to fifty thousand troops were said to be ready to embark from England for New York. If there had been any doubt about what the battle at Breed Hill had meant in June, there could be none now. With one victory at Montreal and one defeat at Quebec, the Americans and British were at war. But in New York Harbor all was quiet and there was no war.

The stalemate continued for months. Clinton arrived to take command of the British early in the new year, while more citizens fled from the city and more militia entered. British control of the harbor made it apparent that New York could not be long defended against any serious attack, but it was decided not to evacuate the city. Provisions were no longer allowed to reach the warships and by April they had left the harbor. When the Declaration of Independence, which Robert Livingston of the up-river estate had helped to draft, was read to the people in July, the tide of sentiment turned sharply and became more consolidated. The statue of the King was overthrown amidst bonfires and speeches and parades. New York was joined with her sister colonies in overt rebellion and independence became a prime aim of the struggle.

Forty-five ships of the Royal Navy had appeared off Sandy Hook at the end of June. Three now sailed up the river past the American batteries as though to demonstrate their weakness. Attemtps to burn the ships failed and they returned nonchalantly to the harbor, where two more fleets joined the first. Loyalists fled to their protection despite guards along the river. Howe arranged a conference with the Americans on Staten Island and offered a pardon couched in language that made it clear that the Crown would not recognize any authority of the Continental Congress. Washington referred the British to that body as the legal government of the colonies, thereby refusing the offer.

On August 22 the British put troops ashore at Gravesend. The Americans were occupying positions along the hills running east and west across upper Long Island. The British executed the simple maneuver of sending some of their forces around the eastern end of the American line, forcing the Americans to fall back to avoid encirclement. The retreat across the East River was made with little loss, thanks to the great skill displayed by Washington coupled with some extremely good luck and the failure of the British to pursue, a circumstance that was to save the Americans again and again during the next six years.

On September 4 the British began rowing troops across the East River at Turtle Bay. Again a large part of the American army was threatened with being cut off in the lower part of Manhattan, and a panic turned retreat into rout. Washington utterly lost his temper with his inexperienced army, riding among them to curse, threaten, and beat them with his horsewhip. He was very nearly taken by the British vanguard as, left behind by the last of the terror-stricken men, he sat his horse, disgusted and ashamed. An aide grabbed the bridle and led Washington and his mount away to the north minutes before the first redcoats came streaming up to what is now 42nd Street.

The British resumed their march up the island. Contemptuous of the rabble they faced, they played fox-hunting airs on their horns. The enraged Americans attacked at the Hollow Way, the valley where 125th Street runs today, and flung the regulars back for the first time. After a two-hour battle at 116th Street, the Americans rushed forward with bayonets and the British broke and fled back to their camps in the woods of what is now upper Central Park, pursued by the reinvigorated rebels.

While one of the most highly individualistic armies the world has ever seen camped in littered disorganization and high spirits on Harlem Heights, New York caught fire. The flames of a thousand burning structures could be seen by Washington's army. Both sides said the other had done the deed, but neither would have profited from it. The British hanged some men and cut the throats of others they suspected of starting the fire. Ruined lower Manhattan became a wretched slum, full of camp followers and shacks, and it was to remain so throughout the British occupation. Two days later Nathan Hale died on a gibbet near the present 55th Street at First Avenue. His career as a spy had been terribly brief, as were his last, fame-bound words.

For a third time the Americans found themselves in danger of being outflanked. The British had the trap all but sprung when they sailed up the East River to the Bronx, but they attempted to land at an unusually defensible spot and spent five days on the long peninsula of Throg's Neck before they re-embarked and tried a wider beachhead. The Americans used the time well in withdrawing to White Plains and taking up advantageous positions where the British would have to attack uphill. Just two months after the battle on Long Island the British charged into action again. Using cavalry extensively, Howe took Chatterton's Hill where the American artillery was stationed and broke the line of defense. The American Army fled northward in defeat, but Howe did not follow. Again the British failed to strike at a decisive moment that might very well have ended the Revolution as an organized armed rebellion.

The final blow fell in November. Hessians attacked Fort Washington, the highly regarded stronghold on the Hudson near the present George Washington Bridge. The commander in chief was again nearly taken. As the attack began he was on his way from Fort Lee, across the river. From a small boat he and Generals Greene and Putnam watched the defeat and capture of almost three thousand men. Washington got his shrinking army across the Hudson and took it south to Hackensack. Before the order to wreck and abandon Fort Lee could be executed, the British fell upon it and entered the fort so closely upon the heels of its recent garrison that the soup in their kettles was still hot.

The war swept away from the city as Washington led his discouraged farmers southwest through New Jersey. It never returned. Howe and the fleet sat in New York and enjoyed the war. The loyalists flocked to the city while the militia fortified the river. Between the two forces Westchester was open to the depredations of either side, and to the independent, bandit-like groups who became known as cowboys, since one of their primary activities was driving off cattle to sell to the armies.

The Revolution divided families as well as land. New York State was one of the strongest Tory centers and its people were torn by bitterness. The success or defeat of one side or the other was often enough to cause the majority to change in a given area. Tories living upon their farms were sometimes unmolested for years. In other cases they were stripped of all they possessed and driven away, threatened with death, or occasionally killed.

Beverly Robinson could not bring himself to support outright rebellion. He retired to his farm across from West Point when hostilities commenced. When the British took New York he returned to the city. But he later went back up to his home, which had become the residence of the commander at West Point, to see that his property was in order. He also intended to try to persuade General Putnam to give up his rebellious ways and return to the service of his king. The general was absent, so Robinson presented his arguments to the general's wife and returned to New York. It was that kind of war.

The next major threat came from the north. Burgoyne marched from Canada to effect a meeting with Howe somewhere on the Hudson. They would cut the colonies in two—the old threat—and then be able to deal with the parts more easily. Schuyler felled trees across his road for miles; Stark killed four hundred of the five hundred Hessians sent out to scare up food in Vermont and Massachusetts; Herkimer and Arnold stopped additional British forces under Leger from advancing down the Mohawk valley from Lake Ontario.

A young girl living at Fort Edward, the daughter of a loyalist, was the fiancée of Captain Jones of Burgoyne's artillery. The young captain feared what might become of her among the wild rebels heading north. He promised two Indians who were serving with the army a barrel of rum if they would bring Jane McCrea to the British camp. On their way back the Indians fought over who should deliver the girl and receive the rum until one of them settled the problem by smashing his tomahawk into her head. The cruelties of the Indian allies of the British had fostered considerable hatred already, and now the whole countryside rose to join the army against Burgoyne.

Gentleman Johnny reached the Hudson in August of 1777, having built forty bridges in the wilderness for his enormous train of troops, baggage, guns, and ladies. There he waited for news of Howe, but that general made no move up the river. Burgoyne pushed on toward Albany. In mid-September he crossed the Hudson, burned General Schuyler's house, and proceeded slowly south. Arnold, begging Gates to attack rather than wait where the British cannon could do their work best, was at last allowed to advance with a part of the large American force. He ambushed Burgoyne and stopped him with a murderous fire for two hours until artillery coming up put heart into the British again. Arnold asked Gates for reinforcements, thinking to end Burgoyne's campaign then and there. Gates refused, although eleven thousand men were idle in the American camp. Arnold held on until dark and then withdrew. Gates had played cards all day while Arnold had fought; as commander, he reported the battle without mentioning Arnold's name. A few days later Gates removed Arnold from command of the troops he had led. The disgusted and outraged Arnold was persuaded to stay with the army by a letter signed by his fellow officers, but he was without official duty.

The Americans waited as did Burgoyne. There was no word from Howe, but Clinton was reported on the move up the Hudson. Burgoyne could not wait any longer; his supplies were too low and the Americans surrounded him so that his troops could not forage. On October 7 he tried to force a way past Gates and the battle was on. Benedict Arnold joined in despite Gates's efforts to stop him and led the Americans in repeated attacks. The British were being overwhelmed when Arnold crashed to the ground from his mount, a ball in his leg. With evening the battle closed. Ten days later the British surrendered and were ferried across the Hudson on the first leg of a journey to Cambridge and prison.

The British had been defeated by inexperience, inflexibility, bungling, and the lack of a real desire to prosecute the war as much as they had been beaten by the American forces. Howe was virtually a gift to America. He was a Whig who either apparently felt a disinclination to win the war or believed that it was not possible, a gentleman much enamored of cities and ladies and a general who, though brave, had experienced the horror of Bunker Hill at first hand. What he had not dared to do with all his army Clinton dared with a mere four thousand men. Too late to be helpful to Burgoyne, he started up the Hudson River with two frigates and a few smaller boats. Cleverly feinting at Tarrytown and Verplanck's Point, he held Putnam's forces south of the Highlands, then landed two thousand redcoats below Dunderberg Mountain. They were guided by a local Tory over the hills to a position behind the two forts guarding the river where it narrowed at Bear Mountain. The Americans inflicted three hundred casualties but had to abandon both Fort Clinton and Fort Montgomery. The British hacked through the huge chain the Americans had placed across the river, and the last of the impregnable defenses were destroyed. Warning fires flamed atop Mount Beacon as the British ships sailed north and terror spread before them. Clinton sailed on, firing cannon at houses along the river and burning some. Kingston was evacuated before the British marched ashore to burn down all the town except for one house. Moving on from this last capital of the rebel colony, they crossed over the river to burn the home of the great landowner, Livingston, and other nearby houses. Clinton now knew of Burgoyne's defeat. His expedition was powerless to change that, but it had brought havoc into the center of New York and Clinton returned down-river satisfied.

Again the long fight moved away from the Hudson toward the south. Finally, twenty months after Saratoga and the destruction of Kingston, Clinton's troops again dashed up the Hudson and took Stony Point on the west shore and Verplanck's Point opposite. Six weeks later General Wayne led troops over the hills and down to Stony Point, reversing the route traveled by Clinton's men on their way to Forts Clinton and Montgomery. At midnight the Americans attacked and took the fortifications. It was a much-needed victory, a decisive blow in a period when all had grown muddled and the war had gone on for a very long time. A month later young Henry Lee stormed the British fort on Paulus Hook across from New York. His five hundred men surprised a sleeping garrison and made off with their prisoners in the night, hotly pursued and nearly caught.

The war dragged on. It seemed clear that the British could not win unless they changed their tactics, but the Americans were desperately tired. Troops were unfed, unclothed, unpaid, and anxious about their homes and families, as they had been for years. Desertions wiped out entire units. Colonel Van Alstyn was supposed to be in command of a regiment guarding the Hudson, but it numbered only the commander and one other man. Van Alstyn therefore experienced a certain uneasiness when he was commanded to march one fourth of his regiment to Fort Arnold.

The credit of the rebels was entirely gone. The French fought with them but their navy had not been able to strike a decisive blow. By 1780 there were many on both sides who wished the war would end at almost any price.

Benedict Arnold, who was unable to assume an active command because of the wound he had received at Saratoga, was military governor in Philadelphia. The old warrior's young Tory bride, Peggy Shippen—to whom he had written, "Our difference in political sentiment will, I hope, be no bar to my happiness"—was in correspondence with the brilliant young Major André, who had been one of her beaux during the British occupation of Philadelphia. Persuaded by the affronts he had borne from commanders who were not his equal, by criticisms from the Congress, and by a recent army trial for the alleged misuse of army matériel, and influenced as well by the ambitions and persistent arguments of Peggy that the Americans' position had weakened so much that they could never now achieve victory, Arnold was at last won over to a betrayal of such importance that it might very well have ended the war. He demanded a more active command, but refused to accept the cavalry and asked Washington again for his first choice, West Point, which was granted. In July of 1780 he and Peggy moved into the Beverly Robinson house in Garrison and Peggy resumed her code letters to André.

The morning after his meeting with André at Haverstraw, Arnold was given a note from Colonel Jameson down in Westchester that said that he held a British spy who bore a pass from the general and suggested that it would be wise to find out who had forged Arnold's name to it. Hamilton was sitting at table with him as he read, and Washington was about to arrive. Arnold excused himself, spoke to his wife privately, and went down to the river where his six-oared barge was kept ready. He had escaped to the British warship *Vulture* before Washington could send out a posse to take him.

The Tory farmer who had been sent with André to guide him down to the British lines had grown fearful about meeting some of the "cowboys" of Westchester and had turned back. André had lost his way after that and had at last been stopped and taken prisoner by some men who would probably have passed him on had he still been in the company of Joshua Smith, whom they knew. The papers he carried and his civilian clothes condemned him. Reluctantly, for he was a young man of great charm and ability, the Americans tried him, found him guilty of spying, and hanged him at Tappan.

Arnold was made a brigadier general in the British Army and raided the coast with uncharacteristic brutality until the end of hostilities. Peggy, unsuspected by all save Aaron Burr, acted her part well and went into exile with her husband. None of her dreams of royal favor, peerage, and wealth materialized.

For the next three years, until the peace, there was no more fighting on the Hudson. After Yorktown, Washington returned to Newburgh and there he waited for the decisions that were being made in France. It was a pleasant time in some ways, with dancing and feasts, skating on the river, and fireworks to relieve the boredom. But the troops wanted to go home. They had to be kept until the war was officially over. British troops still waited just a few miles away. Replying to one protest meeting that had reached fever pitch, Washington stopped in his speech to put on his glasses. "I have grown gray in your service," he said. "Now I am becoming blind." The troops stayed. In December of 1783 he at last rode into New York City, free of the last British troops in the new country.

The new state was very slow to change. New York was controlled by aristocrats until the end of the century, except for those who had remained loyal to the Crown, the same aristocrats who had been in control before the Revolution. Only eighteen per cent of the population qualified to vote in state elections; twelve per cent had held this right before the war. The gradual emancipation of slaves was begun in 1799, but all would not be freed until 1827. There was a long pull ahead for every state, and in New York those who were in a position to lead were generally those who had already been in command, the gentlemen landowners and the clever merchants and lawyers, now further entrenched by the fact that many of them had served their country's cause so long and well.

Before the war the colony of New York had consisted almost entirely of lands along the Hudson; twelve of its fourteen counties bordered the river, the other two making up Long Island. A few outposts were to be found in the Mohawk Valley and even fewer in the north beyond Fort Edward, but the bulk of the population was in the counties along the river. After the Revolution the same was true for quite some time except that the Mohawk became more thickly settled after the Iroquois were removed from their lands, and a scattering of Vermonters crossed over to settle down along the west shore of Lake Champlain. The wilderness of the Adirondacks and the Catskills still confined the good land, and in the north the patriotic Livingstons, Van Rensselaers, Schuylers, and related families had most of it except westward along the Mohawk where the frontier lay.

The estates of those manor lords who had cast their lots with the British were not broken up and distributed to the veterans of the long war as the farmer militia had hoped. They were mostly sold to land speculators and wealthy men who hoped to maintain country estates in their turn. The state was in desperate need of money and through selling off these properties and other large tracts of unclaimed public lands intended to accumulate funds. Of the Philipse domain the southern part, which was known as Yonkers, passed through several hands until it finally came into possession of Lemuel Wells in 1813. When this had been the manor of the Philipses it had consisted of about sixty dwellings, the manor house, a flour mill, a sawmill, a tavern, a church, a fishhouse, and a school. When the estate was broken up after Wells's death in 1842, the only additions were a dozen more dwellings, two schools, a church, an inn, and two stores. Not until then, sixty years after the Revolution, were people able to buy small pieces of this property and begin to build the city of Yonkers.

Until the end of the century, then, New York was still largely a strip of farm land, much of it in the form of great estates along the Hudson, with a city at each end of the populated area. And very modest cities they were, for in all the states in 1800 only 322,000 people were living in cities while almost 5,000,000 lived on farms.

Again and again the chronicles of the eighteenth-century illuminate just how small were the numbers of people who commanded the affairs of the colony and the new state and how frequently their paths intertwined. There were only so many individuals possessing proper qualifications for leadership and social prominence, according to the lights of the period, and these managed to do and be everything of importance. One series of connections by inheritance, marriage, and acquaintance involves several famous names and two famous homes.

Stephanus Van Cortlandt's daughter, Catherine, became the second wife of Frederick Philipse in 1692, while his son, Jacobus, had married Philipse's adopted daughter, Eva de Vries, the year before. Less than a hundred years later the Philipse family were all in England and their estates had been confiscated. The descendants of Eva and Jacobus Van Cortlandt were still in America, however, for the family had been in favor of the rebellion. Eva's son, Frederick, had built the fine house still standing in Van Cortlandt Park in New York, and his granddaughter, Cornelia Van Cortlandt Beekman, became mistress of the Philipse Castle on the Pocantico when her husband bought it after the Revolution.

The last Frederick Philipse who was lord of the manor, great-grandson of the first Frederick, had two sisters, Susannah and Mary. Susannah married Beverly Robinson, of Virginia, whose family were well known to Washington's, and whose house in Garrison was to be the residence of Benedict Arnold while he was briefly in command of West Point. Mary Philipse met George Washington at her sister's New York home when the future commander was a young colonel. According to letters to certain friends, Washington found Mary very attractive and hoped to see her more. But Washington's course lay another way and the popular belle became the wife of another young colonel, Roger Morris, in 1758. Colonel Morris built a handsome home for his bride on the heights of upper Manhattan.

Like his brother-in-law, Roger Morris could not bring himself to rebel against his king and had to abandon his home for the protection of the British-held city when the Revolution began. During the battle of the Hollow Way and for a month after that the Morris house was Washington's headquarters.

Sometime after the Revolution, Washington once conducted a group of people through the house, and among these was his young wartime aide, Alexander Hamilton, now a member of his cabinet. A few years later Hamilton, who lived nearby at the present 140th Street, said good-by to his wife, Betsy Schuyler, much as he did each morning before driving down to his law office in the city, and went to meet Aaron Burr over hot pistols in Weehawken. The Morris house had become a tavern, but it was soon bought by John Jacob Astor and then sold by him to Stephen Jumel, who died in 1832. Aaron Burr, who was practicing law in New York after his European exile, sought the widow Jumel's hand but was put off until one day, bringing a minister with him to the house, he terminated her indecision or reluctance and married her on the spot.

The nineteenth century opened upon a vista of enormous growth and change in the Hudson River valley. New York would expand in this century from a town of some 60,000 people scattered over a few square miles in lower Manhattan Island to a city covering some 260 square miles of land whose population of 2,000,000, long accustomed to climbing five or six flights of stairs to their dwellings and to riding in elevated railways, were now becoming familiar with buildings so tall that the elevators manufactured in Yonkers by Elisha Otis had to be included in their plans.

The river would fast become an ever-busier place in this century, linked to northern and western waters by some of the scores of canals that were enthusiastically constructed early in the century, a superb network of waterways that was thought to be the answer to the demands of the burgeoning economy. The longest canals would be completed in time to be rendered at least partially obsolete by the railways, and many lesser canals would be abandoned within a few years of completion. In America the industrial revolution could flourish as it never had—and never would again—consuming the apparently inexhaustible riches of the New World and the endless supply of man, woman, and child power flowing from the Old. It offered opportunities even to these humble immigrants, and to a handful of men it gave fortune in a degree usually bestowed only upon monarchs. While their Hudson homes spread along the riverbanks, others, fleeing from the challenge and ugliness of the dynamic age, were to try again and again to create utopian communities based upon precepts and ideals that were impossible to implement. The romantic nature of the century found expression, too, in the mists and crags of the Hudson River painters, in the deliberate creation of rustic and picturesque estates and in the evolution of a poetically ritualized and simplified mode of life for those who owned them. As the river boomed toward the twentieth century even its most rapacious barons learned to look another way with nostalgic longing.

The Dutch had developed a sailing vessel, a simple sturdy sloop, modified over the years until it was by far the best means of transport on the river. Two years after the Revolution one of these Hudson River sloops undertook to show the enterprise and seamanship of the new country by sailing to China and back around Cape Horn. The *Experiment* of Albany, with a crew of ten, became the first American ship to sail directly to China. The round trip took eighteen months, achieved its international aim, and firmly established the Hudson River sloop as the nonpareil of the river. Hundreds of them crowded the waters early in the nineteenth-century, and wealthy upstate families made their trips to New York in their own elegant sloops.

Other sails appeared on the Hudson. Nantucket and New Bedford whalers came, seeking a port less exposed to depredations such as they had faced for eight years during the rebellion. They settled upon a site one hundred twenty miles from the mouth of the river and proceeded to found the town of Hudson. Business and the town, which became an official seaport, flourished together. The fleet of whalers grew larger and larger and Hudson missed by one vote the honor of becoming the capital of the state. The embargoes and other complications of the war of 1812 reached out to shut down the whaling of Hudson City as completely as if their ships and homes had been burned by British sailors. Not until 1830 did whaling ships sail again from the river, and now whalers from Poughkeepsie, Newburgh, and New York joined in the chase after the ever-more-distant and scarce leviathan. The depression of 1837, new inventions such as gas lighting, and the underground oil found in Pennsylvania dealt successive blows to the Hudson River whalers and sent the industry into a last decline before mid-century.

For a quarter of a century men had been experimenting with steamboats. Several had made successful test runs on the Hudson—including a screw-propeller model built by the Stevens family at their Hoboken castle—and John Fitch's steamer had made regular runs on the Delaware in 1790. But in 1807 Robert Livingston—once delegate to the Continental Congress, one of the young men who had drafted the constitution of his state, ambassador to France and successful negotiator of the Louisiana Purchase, and the leading member of the family that had ruled for more than one hundred years over their vast up-river estates—had two things in his pocket that would give him control of the Hudson River steamboats. One was Robert Fulton, whose *Clermont,* incorporating the best of several steam-engine designs, promised to win over those who were prejudiced against steam and sweep sailing vessels from the river. Mr. Fulton himself had won the affections of Livingston's daughter, Harriet, and would shortly become a member of his patron's family. Then, second, Chancellor Livingston, whose influence in state affairs was understandably large, had prevailed upon the legislature to assign to himself and the young inventor the sole rights to make and operate steamships upon the waters of the entire state. They might, if they wished, grant this right to others for a fee.

The war of 1812 threatened the young country's prosperity as much as its security. England was busy with Napoleon and made little effort to win the American conflict until after the greater threat was ended. Once again—and for the last time—an enemy tried to force its way down the avenue of conquest, the Champlain and Hudson valleys. The British gained control of Lake Champlain but their fleet was badly defeated by a smaller American navy, after which they withdrew their armies to Canada. The chief effect of the war upon the Hudson was economic. While trade was brought to a halt by the embargoes and hostilities, the price of farm products rose and the inventive and organizational genius of the valley flourished as America was forced to manufacture what had been imported. After the war with Britain tariffs protected the growth of industry, and during the next three decades the area grew phenomenally as an industrial center. The population increased until in 1820 it exceeded that of any other state. A decade later New

York was more populous than all New England. By 1850, with 3,000,000 people it was larger than any two other states in the union. Twenty times as much produce flowed through the newly constructed canals and down the river as had been sent from the West before 1830. New York City was the first port of the nation.

By 1815 both Robert Livingston and Robert Fulton had died. Larger and better steamboats were being built all over the country except on the Hudson, where the heirs of the Livingston-Fulton monopoly allowed only eight boats to operate. In the lower parts of the river where the jurisdiction of New Jersey complicated matters, Cornelius Vanderbilt and others were battling the monopoly with some success, but elsewhere its restrictions held. In 1824 the Supreme Court declared that the monopoly must cease and the shipyards of the river slammed full speed ahead in a race to put more and more boats in the water.

If there was a river made for steamboating it was the Hudson. One twentieth the size of the Mississippi basin rivers, but every bit as wide as most of them, the Hudson offered its magnificent scenery for the passengers who made of each trip aboard the floating palaces an endless social occasion, everyone talking to everyone else with the enthusiasm and dogmatism of the new American. The manufacturing might of the country grew enormously in the Northeast, the village factory being to this area what the cotton gin was to the South and barbed wire to the West— the means to an expanding economy. Along the Hudson factories blossomed in a profusion exceeded only in New England. And the river was wide and deep and straight, free of the hidden hazards of the Western streams—perfect for racing. And race they did, tying down safety valves, cutting the price of tickets to the bone, laying great wagers, stoking furnaces with costly balustrades and gilt furniture, ignoring the increasingly severe prohibitions against the dangerous practice, and regularly blowing up boilers, crashing onto islands or against landings, killing passengers, and providing more excitement than the dull, dirty railways that were creeping up-shore ever could.

But the railways could not be stopped. Lacking the gilt luxury of the steamboats or the crafted grace of the sailing vessels, the ugly, utilitarian, and dangerous trains quickly achieved their purpose. Railroads began as separate and tiny systems, each dependent upon the city in its center and each with a track of different gauge to ensure against its use by another company. Needless to say, growth was impeded by this system of short, radiating roads. Certain powerful men of large vision coupled with small scruples began acquiring, by a colorful variety of means, the rights over railway properties and started to build them into large systems. Again, that ideal of the times, monopoly, was the aim, and in New York State armed men were used in the campaign to achieve it. In 1848 the railway was run up the river's edge to Albany, and although both canals and steamboats still contribute to the life of the river after one hundred years and more of competition with rails, the decline of both as major means of transporting goods and passengers was begun. The chief effect of the canals upon the railroads was the maintenance of low rates. Goods from the West could be carried on the canals for a fraction of what it had cost to bring them East by wagon. When the railroads arrived on the scene they had to meet the established low rates of the canals. Eventually the effect was to keep all rail rates from the West low.

The only earlier method of transportation that was not swiftly superseded by steam engines was the clipper ship. Brought to a beautiful perfection in America, where interest in steamboats did not extend to ocean-going vessels, the fast clipper was recommended over the English-developed steam yachts even by English travel agents; a passage on one of these beautiful ships was so much more pleasant, clean, quiet, and exhilarating than a trip aboard the sooty, graceless steamer. The sailing vessel would not be overtaken by steam in America until the end of the century, but all else—stage, inland sail, steamboat, wagon, and riding horse—was outmoded by the railroad.

It was a time of utopias.

Ann Lee came to the Hudson before the Revolution with her tiny band of faithfuls, already toughened by their treatment in England. These Shakers wandered and preached and could not be stopped by being run out of town, by beatings, or even by being denounced as British agents. In 1792 a community was organized at New Lebanon and a second was shortly set up northwest of Albany. Their doctrine decreed communal ownership, a severely prescribed daily ritual (relieved only by song fests and religious convocations that featured shaking, whirling, hysteria, and speaking unintelligibly), demanded a full day of busyness, a dull and uniform dress, and strict celibacy and separation of the sexes. Still, the Shakers grew in numbers until about the time of the Civil War. For decades they managed their farms efficiently and grew rich from the increasing sales of their plain, excellently made furniture and implements. Then the movement declined and one by one outlying communities were sold as their membership dwindled. Sometimes the few who remained returned to the first settlements to live out their last years. The Shakers built wonderfully well—plain, solid buildings whose proportions are their only ornaments—but none of their structures now exists in the Hudson River area except at New Lebanon, over on the Massachusetts line, and west of Albany, where two of their groups of buildings remain. Here, too, there is a graveyard in which all the stones are identical except for Mother Lee's slightly larger monument, which stands in the center of fifteen rows of thirty stones each and one row of just six—the last of the Shakers.

Peter de Labigerre, having married a Beekman and built a moated Chateau de Tivoli, embarked upon a plan to provide his home on the river with an appropriately lovely town and also to profit from rising land values. His utopia would be one of handsome homes and pleasure gardens along streets named Flora, Diana, Peace, Plenty, and Bargain. Despite the flattery of another street called Chancellor, Robert Livingston foreclosed his mortgage on De Labigerre's lands in 1807. Empty lots on Chancellor Street (and Flora, Plenty, Bargain, etc.) were not flattering at all and they were bad business; the chancellor's money might be better invested in his son-in-law's steamboat that year. Tivoli is still the name of a town on the river, but nothing remains of Peter de Labigerre's Tivoli.

The Owenites established communities along the Hudson, in 1825 at Haverstraw, later at Coxsackie. Anti-religious, gay, based upon Robert Owen's quite rational ideas, which did not admit much room for possible human failure or the persistent snags of emotion, both communities briefly roused shocked opposition and then perished by malfunction. As was usual in reason-inspired utopias, there were too many gentle poets and philosophers, too few workers and farmers, and so much talking and reasoning about the best ways to proceed that no one ever could for long.

In Washington County, north of the Shaker communes, William Miller experienced a revelation that was not infrequent in the early nineteenth century. But somehow the faith aroused by his announcement that all save those who believed with him must soon perish with the world survived despite repeated blows. The first time the date for the holocaust was set farms in Washington County were sold, neglected, or given away. The Millerites gathered atop hills and spent the night in prayer while others came to watch, perhaps not without the thought that they might be near enough to share the Millerites' guaranteed protection if by any chance they knew what they were doing. Most of Miller's followers survived the ridicule of the next morning with enough faith to try again. Dates for this kind of event were arrived at by interpreting and combining various figures mentioned in the Bible (such as the age of Adam or the years of the Babylonian captivity), and Miller had simply made an error in his arithmetic. Next year again, however, a placid, more or less ordinary morning followed a night of fervent prayer, fear, and hope. The Millerites were not daunted. Once more they went over their figures and found the trouble. In 1845 fifty thousand Millerites reorganized as Adventists. Miller died four years later. His utopia has been postponed for quite some time but the Adventists have continued to increase in numbers to this day.

The Perfectionists were one of the long-lasting communities. They had a printing plant and some houses in New York City but their main, bustling community was Oneida, just west of the headwaters of the Mohawk. The leader of the Perfectionists, John Humphrey Noyes, scandalized America by his theory that one of the best ways to experience and express love of God was in the sexual union of a loving pair—any loving pair. His doctrine of multiple marriage remained theory for some years. Not until Mary George convinced him that the time was right did Noyes and the Oneidans practice what they preached.

This prosperous community had no connection with the Hudson except that its members often traveled on it in their trips to New York and back, and through an accident on one of these voyages that left three Perfectionists on its shores forever. Mary George, the persuasive second wife of the leader, joined a group of fellow Perfectionists aboard their sloop to share their labors on a trip to New York and particularly to disperse the increasing gloom of one of them with her cheery ways. The depressed Perfectionist was at the tiller when a sudden gust hit the boat. As she canted, the other men rushed up from the cabin to help and were thrown into the water when the sloop capsized. The ladies were trapped below and drowned. Mary George and her sister Oneidans were recovered and buried just above Hyde Park, still in their Perfectionist bloomers and short skirts.

More acceptable philosophies were preached in the Hudson Valley, some of which swept through the nation in a quick way that was to become a familiar American pattern. Orson Fowler's octagonal house was more than an architectural innovation; its builder knew from his experiences in phrenology that a great many of his country men were more interested in getting to the meaning of life than in merely living it. His books on phrenology had run through as many as forty editions, and the craze for determining what was the real character of one's self and of anyone whose head was within reach of a skillful hand had made Fowler rich and famous. Fowler first wrote a book entitled *A Home for All, or The Gravel Wall and Octagon Mode of Building,* which stressed the subtle, spiritual benefits to be obtained from living in an octagonal house of his design. His plan also included a number of architectural items that were well in advance of his time. Houses built according to his recommendations soon rose all along the river as well as in most of the Northeastern states. There might be many more than the dozen or so still standing in the river valley if Fowler's own house near Beacon had not been made of grout, a mixture of cement, gravel, and sand that the author recommended. This somewhat porous material allowed the central well to become contaminated only a few years after he had completed the house in 1858—long after some of his readers had built their own octagons—and typhoid followed. The fads of phrenology and octagonology died out well before the century.

Quite different ways of life were advocated by two Hudson River men whose names were very much alike and who lived within a few miles of each other on the river at about the same time. Andrew Jackson Davis, a cobbler of Poughkeepsie, set forth his metaphysical doctrine in a book that was esteemed by a New York college professor as "one of the most finished specimens of philosophical argument in the English language." Davis argued that there was no mind, only matter and power, and if one knew the secret of how to apply one's power to matter, as he did, then disease and unhappiness could be banished. Following in the wake of his doctrine—as in the wakes of similar theories that found fertile soil in mid-century society—were reports of marvelous cures, happiness, and heretofore impossible achievements, all manifestations of the newly discovered truths of Andrew Jackson Davis. *Principles of Nature, Her Divine Revelations and a Voice to Mankind* continued to be issued until the 1860's, its author became rich, and the United States Senate gravely listened to Davis when he appeared before it seeking government endorsement and financial support for his methods. But Davis lacked organizational skill and his cult died away while he was still living.

Andrew Jackson Downing, a nurseryman from Newburgh, was much impressed by the romantic ideas of Scott and the Hudson River painters. He was made aware early in his life of the advantages of wealth and culture by his association with certain neighboring Hudson River gentry, especially the Edward Armstrongs, a learned, fashionable, and aesthetic couple who had a beautiful estate at Danskammer Point. Downing soon discovered that his knowledge of planting coupled with well-learned manners and a philosophy of aesthetics expressed with intense conviction could provide a handsome living. He espoused the rustic, particularly for the upland Hudson where, he maintained, formal lawns should be turned into romantic Edens. He became an arbiter of taste, married into the old, aristocratic De Windt family, and set about building his own ideal estate and promoting his ideas on a broader scale by writing books. His poetic gardens with their planned, wild look, their rustic little buildings and bridges, their urns and fountains became popular on the big estates before mid-century.

He urged that New York set aside a large tract in its center for a park. Despite his firm conviction that an aristocracy of the gifted few must not be destroyed by overly democratic theories, he also maintained that the influence of art and nature would elevate all and should be available to all. He was asked by President Fillmore to plan the grounds of the Capitol and the White House. At thirty-seven, at the height of his fame, he and his wife boarded the *Henry Clay* at Newburgh. The steamboat was loaded with three hundred people and was in the midst of a prohibited race down-river against another steamer. Off Riverdale a boiler exploded. The flaming *Henry Clay* was run into the shore at full speed. Eighty people, including Andrew Jackson Downing, died. The next year, 1853, the legislature passed a law that ended the period of steamboat racing on the Hudson.

Downing's horticultural and architectural ideas continued to exert their appeal. The ornate Hudson River bracketed house, a "cottage" style he approved for the area, continued to be built on many estates during the latter half of the century. Central Park was the work of two of Downing's disciples, Calvert Vaux and Frederick Olmsted. Special ruins were built by John Cruger on a point of land overlooking the river and the Clewes family at Hyde Park followed the romantic ideas of Downing to the same logical extreme on their estate. The first of the Hudson's castles began to decorate the tops of hills, and while Andrew Jackson Downing might have thought little of such ostentation it seemed to most people in the valley to be the embodiment of his doctrine.

The painters who influenced Downing were a second wave of Hudson River painters. Their predecessors, a group who are sometimes called the patroon painters, occupied themselves almost entirely in making portraits of prominent colonial persons and their families. These eighteenth-century artists, mostly anonymous Americans, employed a heavy outline, flattened planes, and the emphasis upon pattern typical of the primitive artist, but they apparently derived many of their ideas of proper portraiture from engravings and whatever European paintings they might have seen.

After this the century became more sophisticated and the typical artist was liable to be either a European come to America to execute as many commissions as possible in a few years, or an American determined to be trained in Europe in the grand classical manner or to imitate such training. It was a time of portraits, allegorical landscapes, and the historic military scene.

Early in the nineteenth century the new romantic painting emerged. Unlike other romanticists these men were little concerned with the past but wished to paint what was before their eyes—although, through literary inspiration, the past frequently crept in again. The elegance and formality of the eighteenth-century were discarded for the ideals of Rousseau, for the appeal of the wilderness, and, in America, for a passion to create an imaginative life to match the material advances of the new country. The arts also reflected the widespread yearning to know and understand one's self that was typical of the period.

In 1825 three landscapes painted by Thomas Cole were displayed in New York and were promptly bought by three older established artists. With the discovery of the young itinerant painter who had just found his permanent subject matter in the wilderness of the Northeast and particularly in the Hudson River area, the new school was launched. Cole's success was immediate; within four years he found himself the most prominent American painter except for Washington Allston. Asher Durand and John Casilear, both engravers, turned to painting landscapes. With a few others, and often with the help of their merchant-patron, Luman Reed, these painters soon formed the first wave of what has become popularly known as the Hudson River school. Cole settled by the river in Catskill and his paintings of this area are most typical of the group: slightly melancholy, literary inspirations are combined with precise observation and careful delineation.

The other painters who are usually thought of as members of the Hudson River school— Kensett, Whitredge, Church, Gifford, Cropsey and Bierstadt, to mention a few—were all children when Cole was at the peak of his renown. They grew up among his admirers, some studied with Cole (Church lived in his Catskill home as a young student), and, when they took to painting, they followed along his way for a while. Certain of these artists, particularly Frederick Church and Albert Bierstadt, became famous and extremely successful in their lifetimes. They had great technical facility, and the enormous scientific curiosity of the period drove them toward ever more ambitious efforts, more exact and luminous painting, and, in some cases, to careers as world-scouring observers. Church painted in South America (following the path of the great naturalist, Alexander von Humboldt, and inspired by his scientific descriptions), in Labrador (to paint icebergs), in Europe (for the Alps) and in the Middle East (to paint landscapes and amass materials that he later incorporated in his home, Olana Castle).

Had any of these painters persisted in actually painting what was before him, he might very well have become the first American painter who could be considered a major artist. Often their sketches indicate freshness, the individuality, talent, and training sufficient for a master painter, but for one reason or another—the introduction of labored and sentimental symbolism, the imposition of a grand scheme, overly fussy details—their paintings rarely, if ever, succeed in rising above the best second-rate level. Their impact upon America was enormous, however. Interest in science and art was naturally keen at this point of economic and social maturity, but it was even further whetted by the self-conscious knowledge that every American worth his cultural salt *should* be fascinated by the frenzied activity on every side. The Hudson River painters succeeded admirably in supplying the demand for an art to match Yankee ingenuity and drive.

Other artists lived on the Hudson—many of them—but, like most of the writers, inventors, musicians, scholars, or statesmen who lived and live along its banks, few of them have turned to the river for subject matter. Painting was becoming less regional—like inventing—and American writers of note turned from philosophy and politics almost directly toward the beginnings of the characteristically introspective themes of the latter nineteenth-century. Melville and Whitman, in New York, focused their imaginations upon the soul, the conscience, the new freedoms, and the future, although Whitman also sang the praises of Manhattan and the East River. Washington Irving's comic fables of the river Dutch are almost the only literature of the Hudson. Historians have, of course, included its events in their works and Carl Carmer's book is an admirable and romantic account of this saga, but there has been no Faulkner for Columbia County and no Sandburg for Saratoga.

The champion of the common people, George Clinton, had died in 1812. At the start of the Revolution the six-foot-four country lawyer from Newburgh rose to prominence as a fiery patriot, a general with a fine faith in his cause and a persuasive ability that brought upstate farmers pouring into the militia. Elected governor just before Burgoyne launched his invasion in 1777, he held office for eighteen consecutive years despite the opposition of the aristocracy. After again winning the office for a three-year term in 1801 he was elected vice-president and left the political struggles of the state.

Despite the loss to democracy represented by his death the political and economic lot of the common man in the state continued to improve in the first decades of the nineteenth-century, thanks largely to the competition of increasing opportunities in the West, the rise in farm prices and the boom in manufacturing stimulated by the war of 1812, and, finally, the pressure of an increasing popularity of Jacksonian ideals. By 1821 most white males were entitled to vote in

232

the state. In 1836 Martin Van Buren, the lawyer from Kinderhook, became president, chosen as his successor by Andrew Jackson, another sign of increasing equality for all that was fulfilled by Van Buren's identification with the radical wing of the Democratic Party. Judges were now elected rather than being appointed. In short, the river was marching along with the state and the nation toward a more fully democratic life.

The tenants of the Van Rensselaers and Livingstons and other manor lords were left out of this progress. Living on the land their families had occupied for generations, they still were not allowed to own it but had to lease their property, as their forefathers all had been forced to do, by giving a part of their yield to the lord of the manor each year. The descendants of the first Dutch patroon and the first English proprietor refused to sell land; the tenant-farmer system was a profitable one that virtually ran itself after decades of practice. It looked as though a second battle for independence would have to be waged in Rensselaer and Columbia counties.

In 1839 Stephen Van Rensselaer died and his heirs set about trying to collect back rents from their tenants. Rioting broke out, sheriffs were jeered and jostled, auctions of farms for back rent were stopped by threatening mobs. Men armed with rifles and pitchforks and disguised by long calico dresses and masks began drilling and holding meetings in backwoods areas. Their tin trumpets sounded over the hills to call for aid or to play the continual threat to law officers and their posses. A few people were killed and, when young Dr. Smith Boughton was taken prisoner from the midst of a meeting of the insurgents and a crowd of thousands of sympathetic spectators and brought to Hudson, troops began to pour into that city, which the down-renters threatened to burn. No one, it seemed, could identify Dr. Boughton as a leader of the rebels and he was released on bail after a jury failed to reach a verdict in his trial. All had grown quiet, the troops had returned to Albany and New York, and possibly time and talk would settle matters rather than violence. But the summer saw more tarrings and threats.

At Dr. Boughton's second trial the judge made no pretense of his prejudices against the tenants. In his opening address he told them that neither the law nor violence could change their conditions; they must wait for the force of public opinion to bring them justice. John Van Buren, son of the Hudson valley man who in a few years would try to become president again with the slogan, "Free soil, free speech, free labor, and free men," prosecuted the case as the state attorney general. At the close of the sensational trial, which filled the court with the fashionable and the curious, Dr. Boughton was sentenced to life imprisonment. The farmers had lost to the landlords again.

But in the election of the next year, 1846, John Young, who despite being a Whig was sympathetic to the down-renters, soundly beat the Democratic Governor Wright, who had called out the troops to uphold the law. At once Governor Young pardoned Dr. Boughton and a new state constitution was adopted under which the feudal pattern of two centuries came to an end.

The Civil War stimulated the North—and the Hudson River—in much the same way as the war of 1812 had done. Industry took another leap forward, inventiveness became postively rampant, and the wealth of the area increased to such a point that it began to be thought by some that extravagance in this direction might eventually become a problem, even undesirable if, as seemed likely, so much wealth and power were to continue in the hands of so few. By 1870 the wealth of New York State was more than twice as great as the wealth of all the recently defeated Confederate states, yet only about 275,000 of its people earned more than one thousand dollars per year. A new plutocracy emerged, the antecedents of today's corporations and foundations, whose wealth was derived from national and world-wide sources. The only violence to result from the war was a few days of riots protesting the draft in New York, during which the mobs burned buildings, assaulted arsenals and charged police and troops, and were finally herded back to muttering order. The Civil War had eliminated the weak and strengthened the mighty, and it faced the Hudson River toward the modern world.

A few more events must be noted as particular and unique, however. In 1876 Samuel Tilden was elected President of the United States by popular vote and was about to become the second President from the Hudson River area until the Electoral College and a specially appointed electoral commission gave the post to Hayes by one vote. Tilden had lost but he had a magnificent bargain in Yonkers. John Waring had spent a million dollars bringing his "Greystone" estate almost to completion. Financial troubles forced him to sell and Tilden's offer of one hundred fifty thousand dollars was accepted.

When Pierre Lorillard—whose great-grandfather, Pierre I, was the first man to be described by the new term "millionaire"—built Tuxedo Park, he decided to allow membership in his seven-thousand-acre town-club only to a very few leaders of society. In 1886, when Tuxedo Park opened, there were just twenty-two turreted "cottages" and a membership list that included William Astor, Herbert Pell, Ogden Mills, Auguster Schermerhorn, and Pierre Lorillard and son, but did not include his neighbor, the railway magnate, Edward Henry Harriman. With his banker, James Stillman, Harriman thereupon decided to build his own counter-exclusive club at Storm King Mountain. It never had the effect he intended. Tuxedo Park became a symbol of ultra-society and it still exists, exclusive but not eminent, while the Storm King enterprise is today a few foundation rocks on the crest of a hill upon which a modern house is being built.

The country's riches were being accumulated by many individuals from the Hudson River area—New York and Philadelphia had become the outstanding centers of business and finance—but the sources of their wealth were elsewhere. Vanderbilt, Morgan, Harriman, Gould, Belmont, Holley, Hewitt, Schwab, Frick, and many other New York men were titans of finance and industry, but, aside from their social and architectural triumphs and disasters, which ranged from Fifth Avenue to Tivoli, their efforts ranged over the entire land and their stories had escaped from the regional into national and international scope.

The utopian project and the specialized community lost popularity as the confidence of the nation in its destiny rose. Instead of cities of love and equality and reason, the estates of these men who had made fortunes in the boisterous economic expansion grew in number along the Hudson until higher taxes for the rich and higher wages for the workers stopped the further construction of forty-room cottages and summer castles early in the twentieth century. The cost of baronial living continued to rise and wealth sometimes vanished as quickly as it had been amassed in times of depression or panic. The estates began to be sold.

Religious organizations bought scores of the great houses overlooking the river and converted them into schools, retreats, convents, monasteries, homes, chapels, orphanages, and hospitals. Father Divine owns more than twenty properties along the river, including five miles at Crum Elbow. The Roman Catholic Church owns more land in the valley than any other, but

Episcopal properties are also numerous and many other denominations maintain orphanages, summer camps, and schools in the large Gothic, Louis XV, or Victorian houses, and many secular organizations also occupy former mansions. After a lapse of decades since the last attempt at planned communal living, the declining fortunes of a few have given over a very large part of the shores of the Hudson to various specialized communities.

The Adirondacks had been so well, if belatedly, discovered as a large unexploited area that the booming lumber industry, land speculators, and the growing numbers of sportsmen and their often elaborate camps threatened them with the complete exploitation that was so much a part of the American scene after the Civil War. Toward the end of the century the protests of zealous naturalists and conservationists were reinforced by the concern of the rich sportsmen who had found the sort of wild area they needed for rest and recreation along the upper Hudson. The legislature declared the area a park and forest preserve in 1892 and later reinforced the law to make certain that it would remain forever wild. The tide had changed; from this point on there would be increasing agitation for and success in keeping various areas along the river from blight or destruction.

The advent of the automobile was the true symptom of modern times, involving as it does the low cost and identical patterns of mass manufacture, swift mobility, and the financial support of the state in providing it with roadways. The automobile was the penultimate in untrammeled transportation, the complete break away from the rivers and valleys—which even the rails had not entirely achieved. It was only when the demands of the motorist were felt through the land that the bridges over the lower Hudson were built. A corporation headed by Harriman raised money for the first bridge at Bear Mountain. In swift succession the state built the Mid-Hudson and Rip Van Winkle bridges while New York City constructed the George Washington Bridge and the Holland and Lincoln tunnels. Today, with one more bridge at Kingston and another about to replace the ferry at Newburgh, with all but one or two of the ferries that once crossed the harbor waters gone, the river is less and less a barrier. One no longer must interrupt a journey with an often delightful pause on the river.

While the last vestige of the physical Hudson disappears into the gloom of deep water a hundred miles off shore, the historical Hudson rises through layers of time until we no longer think of it as a river of history, but the river of our fathers' memories and our own, clear and familiar. But it is not familiarity with the Hudson that obscures the importance of contemporary events; the river has been removed from the position of historical importance that it once undeniably held. In part, this is true of any river in an area whose techniques of production and communication are ever more independent of geographic features. In an atomic age water is not a prime source of power; in a jet age water is neither the luxurious nor swift roadway; in a missile age water is neither defensive barrier nor dangerous opening; in a metropolitan age water may not be even clean.

Once a handful of men might build a fort and decide the future of a river. Today half a million may build Fords on the same river with less effect upon its history.

c. 1000	Ericsons explore northeast coast.
c. 1350	First Iroquois from west invade Algonquin lands of New York.
1524	Verrazano reports existence of Hudson River to Francis I, King of France.
1540	French traders located at Castle Island (Albany).
c. 1580	Mohawks, driven from Canada by Algonquins, build fortified towns on Mohawk River. Iroquois Confederation formed.
1609	Hudson explores river. Champlain exploring Lake Champlain, attacks Mohawks.
1611	Hendrick Cristiansen and Adrien Block explore Hudson River.
1613	Manhattan Island settled.
1614	Fort Nassau erected (later Fort Orange).
1615	Champlain attacks Oneidas; French-Iroquois enmity decided.
1617	Treaty of Tawasentha: peace between Dutch and Indians firmly established.
1623	Thirty families, mostly Walloons, to New Netherlands.
1625	45 people to New Netherlands, total population over 300.
1626	Peter Minuit, Director General, buys Manhattan for 60 guilders. Indian war drives settlers from Beverwyck (Albany).
1630	Rensselaerwyck established. Michael Pauw's patroonship of Pavonia granted: Staten Island and nearby New Jersey.
1631	600-ton *New Netherlands* launched, largest ship built in Manhattan for next 200 years.
1633	First English ship in river, to Albany to trade. Forced to leave.
1637	700,000 acres in Rensselaerwyck. Pavonia charter bought back by West India Co.
1638	Free trade in the colony proclaimed.
1640	Tappan, Dobbs Ferry, Tarrytown, Kinderhook, Waterford settled. Mohawks, given 400 guns, subdue adjacent tribes, attack French. English at Hartford, eastern Long Island, refuse Dutch entry to Connecticut R.
1642	Fort Crailo built. Director Kieft forms council of 12, agitates for war on Indians.
1643	Mohawks drive river Indians to Pavonia, Manhattan. Director Kieft's soldiers massacre 120. Tribes rise, settlers flee to Manhattan. Hutchinson family killed.
1645	Peter Stuyvesant Director General. Over 2000 in colony.
1646	Van Slyck grant, "Land of Katskill." Brueckelen becomes a village.
1647	Stuyvesant renames Manhattan New Amsterdam. Council elected.
1649	Long Island divided between Dutch and English. Stuyvesant jails, exiles critics.
1652	Stuyvesant declares Beverwyck independent of Rensselaerwyck, arrests director of Rensselaerwyck, destroys houses around fort.
1653	New Amsterdam a city. New Netherlands Congress protests Stuyvesant's rule. Adriaen Van Der Donck charter granted.
1654	English take fort at Hartford. First Jews in New Amsterdam.
1655	Indians attack, kill 100, take 150 prisoners, clear entire area south of Beverwyck to Manhattan of settlers.
1659	Murder looses Indian attack upon Esopus (Kingston), continues through next year.
1661	Schenectady founded. Bergen becomes a village. Treaty of commerce with Virginia.
1663	Stuyvesant urges union with New England for defense. Eastern Long Island declares independence. Mohawk-Mohican war ravishes upper east shore of river.
1664	Richard Nicolls takes New Netherlands for England.
1666	1500 French and Indians burn all Mohawk castles.
	[Patroon painters flourish, 1660-1710.]
1671	Manor of Fordham. First postal route New York to Boston.
1673	Dutch forces retake New York.
1674	Peace treaty returns New York to England.
1675	Gov. Andros visits Mohawks, sets up Board of Indian Affairs, Livingston secretary.
1676	Senate House, Kingston.
1677	Huguenots settle New Paltz.
1680	Coopers organize first "union," agree to charge fixed price for labor; fined 50 shillings each.
1682	Frederick Philipse builds manor houses.
1683	Gov. Thomas Dongon appoints a council of 10, provincial assembly elected; both to consult with governor, meet every three years. All freeholders to have free vote.
1686	Albany a city. Robert Livingston granted patent. King James repeals Charter of Liberties, discontinues general assembly. Ownership of printing press outlawed.
1687	Pelham Manor grant to Thomas Pell.
1689	Jacob Leisler's independent government in New York. King William's War begins. Iroquois attack Canada.
1690	Schenectady destroyed by French and Indians. Albany and Kingston join Leisler regime. First Colonial Congress called by Leisler in New York.
1691	Gov. Sloughter arrives, appointed by King William. Leisler surrenders and is hanged. Poughkeepsie settled.
1693	French again destroy Mohawk castles. William Bradford sets up first press in New York. Philipse patent granted.
1697	Van Cortlandt Manor, Morrisania patents granted. Trinity Church founded. Company including notables of colony formed to break up piracy hires Capt. William Kidd.
1701	Scarsdale Manor to Caleb Heathcote.
1709	Newburgh settled by Palatinate Germans.
1710	First post office, New York. 3000 Germans settle up-river: Germantown, West Camp.
1712	19 Negroes executed on suspicion of plot to burn New York.
1713	Tivoli and Barrytown established.
1719	DeLancey Mansion (Fraunces Tavern).
1725	First newspaper, William Bradford's New York *Gazette*.

1727 John Mynderte wins suit against Albany Council restrictions of trade with Indians. Trade thereafter open to all, boom starts.

1730 Stage line to Philadelphia. Colony still ⅔ Dutch. Livingston builds Clermont.

1731 First fire department. First public library.

1734 Peter Zenger wins trial for libel. Sons of Liberty formed.

1740 King George's War begins.

1741 William Johnson locates at Amsterdam. Second "Negro plot"; 11 burned, 18 hanged, 50 transported from New York.

1745 Saratoga destroyed by force of 500 French and Indians, Washington County ravaged.

1749 William Johnson builds Fort Johnson.

1751 Cadwallader Colden's *Principles of Action in Matter*.

1754 French and Indian War begins. King's College. Albany Post Road completed. Benjamin Franklin's plan for a union adopted at Albany convention rejected by Assemblies.

1755 Staten Island Ferry. Ft. Ticonderoga (Fr.). Ft. Edward and Ft. William Henry (Eng.). Johnson Commissioner of Indian Affairs.

1756 Census reports 97,000 in colony, 71,000 in Hudson River counties. 13,500 are Negroes. Indians are not counted.

1757 Fort William Henry taken by Montcalm.

1759 English take Ticonderoga, Crown Point, Quebec surrenders to Wolfe.

1760 Montreal surrenders. George III. Repressive trade laws reinstated.

1765 Quartering Act. Stamp Act. Mobs take over New York City. Colonial Congress meets in New York, issues Declaration of Rights. Jumel Mansion built by Roger Morris.

1766 Stamp Act repealed. Liberty pole cut down by soldiers. Tenant rebellion, led by William Prendergast, Westchester to Albany.

1770 General committee of 100 formed. Third liberty pole cut down, fight between citizens and soldiers. Fifth pole, remains until 1776.

1771 William Tryon governor. Colony, 168,000; N.Y.C., 22,000.

1774 New York Tea Party. Great Meeting on the Common addressed by Alexander Hamilton. William Johnson dies.

1775 Most Mohawks migrate to Canada with Col. Guy Johnson. Patriot Assembly in New York, Tory-dominated Assembly in Albany. Sons of Liberty seize British vessels and arsenal. First U.S. submarine built by David Bushnell, attempts to blow up British ship. Ticonderoga and Crown Point taken. Citizens prevent removal of British arms. *Asia* bombards New York. Montgomery takes Montreal, is killed at Quebec.

1776 Thomas Paine's *Common Sense*. Schuyler disarms Tories of Mohawk area. Plot against Washington's life, New York. Declaration of Independence read in New York. British land on Staten Island, conferences there fail. Battle of Brooklyn Heights. Execution of Nathan Hale. Battle of Harlem Heights. Battle of White Plains.

1777 State Convention and Constitution at Kingston. George Clinton becomes governor. Stark ambushes Hessians at Bennington. Burgoyne defeated at Saratoga. Gen. Henry Clinton takes Highland forts, burns Kingston, Clermont, returns to New York.

1779 West Point and Constitution Island fortified. Verplanck, Stony Point taken by British. Wayne retakes Stony Point.

1780 Arnold conspires with André to betray West Point. Carleton raids Washington and Saratoga counties.

1783 American Army enters New York City.

1785 Stage line to Albany from New York.

1788 *Federalist Papers*. State Convention ratifies Constitution. New York City made capitol of United States.

1789 Washington takes office. Tammany founded.

1790 State population, 340,000; New York City, 33,000.

1795 Union College. Paine's *Age of Reason*. George Clinton, governor 18 years, succeeded by John Jay.

1797 Albany state capital. Lindenwald built.

1801 Aaron Burr Vice-President. George Clinton again Governor.

1802 West Point Academy. Robert Livingston, Minister to France, and Monroe negotiate Louisiana Purchase.

1803 New York City Hall begun.

1804 Freedom of press increased when Harry Croswell and the Hudson *Wasp* are cleared of criminal libel upon President Jefferson. Burr-Hamilton duel. Clinton Vice-President. John Stevens operates twin-screw steamboat in Hudson.

1805 Fulton builds marine torpedo. Free school opens in N.Y.C.

1807 Fulton's *Clermont*. College of Physicians and Surgeons. Embargo spurs smuggling.

1808 Stevens' ocean-going steamship to Philadelphia.

1809 Washington Irving's *History of New York*.

1815 Daniel Tompkins Vice-President.

1817 De Witt Clinton Governor.

1819 Irving's *Sketchbook*. Emma Willard School.

1821 Troy Female Seminary, first women's high school.

1822 Champlain Canal completed.

1824 Rensselaer Polytechnic Institute. Lafayette in New York.

1825 Erie Canal completed. De Witt Clinton Governor third time.

1826 Hudson River Day Line inaugurated.

1827 Slavery abolished in New York State.

1828 Delaware and Hudson Canal constructed.

1831 Mohawk and Hudson railroad, Albany to Schenectady. Edgar A. Poe's *Poems*.

1832 Joseph Henry transmits electric signals over a wire for more than a mile. New York University.

1833 Van Buren Vice-President. Knit goods manufactured, Cohoes.

1834 New York populace empowered to elect mayor; election and abolition riots. Beginnings of Troy collar and shirt industry.

1835 Great fire in New York.

1836 Martin Van Buren elected President. Manufacture of cotton cloth at Cohoes.
[Hudson River school of painting flourishes, beginning with acclaim for Thomas Cole after 1825]

1837 Samuel F. B. Morse abandons painting to experiment in telegraphy and devise code.

1838 William Seward Governor.

1839 Death of Stephen Van Rensselaer, anti-rent riots start in several up-river counties.

1841 Fordham University. Greeley's *Tribune*.

1842 Croton aqueduct completed. Barnum's American Museum opens.

1844 Morse's telegraph. State Teachers College.

1845 Smith Boughton convicted as leader of anti-rent farmers in Hudson.

1846 New state constitution ends tenant system. Boughton pardoned.

1849 Astor Place riots over British *vs.* American actor (Edwin Forrest), 34 killed. Hamilton Fish Governor. Jenny Lind in New York.

1851 Erie R.R., New York-Dunkirk. Hudson River R.R., New York-Albany.

1852 Elisha Otis invents passenger elevator. A. J. Downing and 80 others die in steamboat explosion, Riverdale.

1855 Largest steamship yet, *Adriatic,* launched in New York. Whitman's *Leaves of Grass.*

1858 First world fair in U.S., Crystal Palace, N.Y.C. First Atlantic cable to Europe completed by Cyrus Field. Design of Central Park undertaken by Olmsted and Vaux.

1859 Cooper Union. Death of Washington Irving.

1860 Bard College. New York State, 381,000; N.Y.C., 800,000.

1861 Vassar. Mayor Wood urges secession of New York. 10,000 troops leave for Washington, isolated by Confederates.

1863 Draft riots in New York, 1000 casualties.

1864 First Bessemer converter, Troy. Confederate conspiracy to burn New York. 22% of Union forces and 42% of money raised for Civil War from New York State.

1866 Cyrus Field uses *Great Eastern* to lay Atlantic cable, replacing first broken cable.

1867 Vanderbilt consolidates New York Central and Hudson River railroads. William Seward acquires Alaska for U. S.

1869 Jay Gould and James Fisk attempt to corner gold, precipitate Black Friday panic.

1870 Stevens Institute. Metropolitan Museum.

1871 Henry Draper's first successful photograph of star, Hastings. David Field's *A Draft Outline of an International Code.*

1874 Samuel Tilden wins presidency by popular vote, loses Electoral College vote. Electric streetcar in New York. Compulsory education law enacted. Nast cartoons expose Tweed ring.

1878 Elevated railway in New York.

1880 Chester A. Arthur Vice-President.

1881 Garfield assassinated, Arthur President.
[Albert Pinkham Ryder, painter, does bulk of work in New York, 1873-1900. Augustus St. Gaudens, sculptor, works in New York during same time.]

1883 Brooklyn Bridge. West Shore Railroad.

1885 Governor Grover Cleveland resigns to become President.

1886 Tuxedo Park opens. Statue of Liberty. General Electric locates at Schenectady.

1890 Ellis Island becomes immigration center.

1893 Edison's Kinetoscope first shown, N.Y.C.

1895 N.Y. Public Library formed from Astor and Lenox libraries.

1898 Greater New York City formed, population 3,400,000.

1900 Theodore Roosevelt Vice-President.

1901 President McKinley assassinated, Roosevelt President. First Poughkeepsie regatta.

1904 New York subway opens. T. Roosevelt elected for second term.

1906 Charles Evans Hughes Governor.

1910 Glen Curtiss flies from Albany to N.Y.C.

1911 Triangle Fire, New York, brings demand for better conditions of employment.

1915 Russell Sage. Black Tom munitions explosion, New York Harbor.

1918 State Barge Canal system. Alfred E. Smith Governor.

1920 Eugene O'Neill receives first of three Pulitzer prizes. Wall Street bomb.

1922 Skidmore. Station WGY, Schenectady.

1924 Storm King Highway. Bear Mountain Bridge and Castelton Railway Bridge.

1927 Holland Tunnel opens.

1928 Franklin D. Roosevelt Governor.

1930 Sacandaga Reservoir completed. Ship channel from Hudson to Albany 27' deep, Albany becomes seaport. Mid-Hudson Bridge.
[John Marin paints New York City intermittently, 1910-35. A. Stieglitz's painting and photography shows foster modern art in first decades of century.]

1931 George Washington Bridge. Empire State Building. Rockefeller Center begun.

1932 Franklin D. Roosevelt President. Herbert Lehman Governor. Nobel Prize in chemistry to Irving Langmuir.

1935 Rip Van Winkle Bridge opens.

1937 Lincoln Tunnel opens. Nobel Prize in Physics to C. J. Davisson and L. H. Genner.

1939 World's Fair in New York.

1940 F. D. Roosevelt first third-term president.

1942 *Normandy* burns. Thomas Dewey Governor.

1945 F. D. Roosevelt dies, buried at Hyde Park.

1949 Brooklyn Battery Tunnel completed.

1952 John Dewey dies. New York exceeds 8,000,000. United Nations at New York.

1957 Kingston-Rhinecliff Bridge.

1959 Guggenheim Museum opens.

1960 Stevens Castle demolished. Narrows Bridge begun.

INFORMATION ABOUT THE PHOTOGRAPHS

in order of most use

cameras Mamiyaflex with f2.8 80mm lens and f4.5 135mm lens
Rolleiflex with f3.5 lens
Nikon SP with f2 50mm lens and f2.5 35mm lens

films Verichrome Pan, Ilford Pan

developers Microdol, FR X-500

papers Velour Black, Varigam, Kodabromide

filters Polaroid, K2, G, A

Most exposures were those that would commonly be indicated for outdoor scenes, except that in general film speeds were assumed to be greater than those indicated by the manufacturers. The great majority of exposures were made with openings from f11 to f22 and at shutter speeds ranging from 1/50 to 1/250. Exceptions:

pp. 48-9 Warrensburg. Late in day. f8 at 1/25.

68-9 Barns. f16 Shutter speed of 1/25 to record falling snow.

74-5 Drying shed. f11, 1/25 to record some detail within shed. As in many instances a great deal of over- and underexposure was required in the printing.

90-1 Sunset at Hudson. f5.6, 1/50.

96-7 Frederick Church studio. f11, 1/50, forced development.

100-1 Catskill Mountain House. Late in day. f16, 1/10.

121 Vanderbilt interiors. f3.5, 1/25, slight overdevelopment.

126 Mid-Hudson Bridge at night. Several exposures were made from f11, 1/25 to f8, 5 seconds. Print giving effect of right hour dependent upon exposure time in enlarger and paper contrast as much as film exposure.

134 Bannerman's Island. Dawn with heavy fog blanket perhaps one hundred feet above the river. f5.6, 1/50.

162-3 Philipse Castle. Ordinary exposures but lights used.

166-7 Lighthouse. About twenty minutes after sunset. f11, 1 second.

170-1 Leaf burning. f4.5, 1/50.

188 George Washington Bridge at night. Negative made from 35mm Ektachrome transparency.

195 Hamilton monument. Dawn with sun barely piercing clouds and haze. f8, 1/50.

202-3 Tugboats in East River at night. f2.5, 1/25.

Several pictures consist of two or three negatives; more than one camera position was sometimes required to record long vistas or large objects that could only be photographed at rather close range. These were all made with the camera hand-held (once overhead, once from a ladder, once from a tower, and once from a small boat) and the inaccuracies of matching were compensated for in the enlarging.

239